NEW PROSPECTS
FOR RETARDED CITIZENS

New prospects for retarded citizens

Pembridge Information Exchange
Session Reports
First Series

Editor: E R Tudor-Davies

**National Society for Mentally
Handicapped Children**

Pembridge Hall,
Pembridge Square, London W2 4EP

© National Society for Mentally Handicapped Children 1975

ISBN 0 855 37031 9

Copies of this publication available from:
NSMHC Bookshop, Pembridge Hall, Pembridge Square, London W2 4EP

Price £4.00

Printed by Green & Co (Lowestoft) Ltd, Crown St., Lowestoft.

Contents

Preface

We are happy to make available to all who must plan future provisions for mentally retarded citizens the experience of those who have long been concerned with their care, and the ideas and plans for improvements, both current and projected in this field.

The Society is much indebted to Dr Guy Wigley and Mr Ali Baquer for their guidance on the design and conduct of the sessions and to the distinguished session editors who all gave so freely of their time to enable a systematic record of the work to be made.

In compiling and editing the reports, E. R. Tudor-Davies has made a significant addition to the information now available to all the disciplines involved. I am sure the book will receive the attention it deserves.

GEORGE W. LEE
Secretary-General
National Society for Mentally
Handicapped Children

Introduction

As every newspaper reader knows there are two kinds of information; news and comment.

This book is the outcome of a new and experimental method of information collection, the Pembridge Information Exchange. New, in that emphasis is on news rather than comment, on fact rather than opinion. Most of the information has been contributed by practitioners working with the retarded in their everyday lives. These participants represent most of the caring services, both statutory and voluntary, and each participant is identified, as also is each reference to the relevant literature, by page and line number in the lists following the report of each of the sessions. In this way it is hoped that other workers, both at home and overseas, will be encouraged to follow-up and benefit, by direct contact, from the work that is at present in progress, and the work that has already been done here in the United Kingdom, in creating new prospects for retarded citizens, both children, adults, and their families.

Pembridge Information Exchanges originated out of the need to obtain, in a rapidly changing environment, effective current information on services for the retarded. In 1972 George W. Lee, Secretary-General to the National Society for Mentally Handicapped Children, approved the launching of the first exploratory sessions, which were held on a regional basis. The idea was to get beyond the seminar or conference, with platforms and speakers, and to seek instead to provide an open forum where professional people could meet together and tell each other what they were doing. A professional worker from the field central to the chosen topic would act as the Editor at each session.

The experiment was inspired by the work of Revans and Baquer. In 1969 Professor R. Revans, with the assistance of Mr Ali Baquer, undertook a project for the Hospital Centre, designed to collect information on the co-ordination of services for the mentally retarded in seven local authority areas. Their Report[1], completed in 1972, indicated that the latest information on paper did not necessarily tally with the latest developments in practice; also, that a useful way to discover the reality of a new development was to get the people doing it to examine what they were doing, by devising their own questions, and as a spin-off from this process, by telling each other what they were doing, perhaps to change the way the thing itself was being done. It was from these beginnings that Pembridge Information Exchanges were launched under the research guidance of Ali Baquer himself, and with Dr Guy Wigley, Medical

Adviser, Inner London Education Authority, as the Adviser to the overall series. In the season 1973/1974 there were nine sessions, each lasting one day. They were held at Pembridge Hall, London, the National Headquarters of the NSMHC.

The organisation and structure of a typical session has been fully described elsewhere[2], and the interaction of participant's contributions lead, from time to time, not only to the provision of information which may not yet be identified in the standard literature, but also to information which might not otherwise have been collected by more conventional methods. Some of these original contributions have been summarised in 'An assessment of the latest developments in the fields associated with mental retardation'.[3] One Editor, a clinical psychologist, responsible for a session on social training and social competence, said of the information exchanges: 'All preconceived ideas that I harboured were swiftly dispelled at the end of the day. It is only through action participation that one realises how often we talk at cross-purposes'.

For those who may wish to adapt Pembridge Information Exchanges to other fields of information collection a useful paper has recently been prepared by Ali Baquer[4] outlining the basic principles of participative research, whilst the open-ended non-directive approach has been clearly set out in the studies of Dr T. R. Batten[5], arising mainly from his work associated with community development, at the University of London Institute of Education.

The use of the methods described above in research and in management should not be confused with their use as an original method of information collection. Specific problems are likely to arise in research and management which do not apply to the collection of information. Students of the information sciences, who may wish to study this matter further, may find a useful guide in the summary of systems theory, particularly as it applies to social work, provided by Irma Stein.[6]

London, 1976.   E. R. TUDOR-DAVIES

1. REVANS, R. and BAQUER, A.   'I thought they were supposed to be doing that' (1972) Hospital Centre: London.
2. TUDOR-DAVIES, E. R.   'In practice': Pembridge Information Exchanges (1974) 'Community Care' No. 28, October.
3. TUDOR-DAVIES, E. R.   'An assessment of the latest developments in the fields associated with mental retardation': Report of the National Spring Conference on Mental Retardation. Exeter University (1975) NSMHC: South West Region.
4. BAQUER, A.   'Innovation in participation' (1975) Chief Executive's Department: London Borough of Greenwich.
5. BATTEN, T. R. and BATTEN, M.   'The non-directive approach in group and community work' (1967) Oxford University Press.
6. STEIN, I.   'Systems theory, science and social work' (1974) The Scarecrow Press Inc., Metuchen: NJ, USA.

IMPROVING THE HOME ENVIRONMENT

Session Editor: Dorothy M Jeffree, M Ed
Research Fellow and Project Director, Hester Adrian Research Centre,
Manchester University

The present situation

Working with parents of the growing child: Manchester University

Dorothy Jeffree believes parents are an important part of the home environment. Her work has been mainly associated with parental involvement and language facilitation projects. It has included the organisation of workshops to provide training in child management, observation and teaching. The aim has been to benefit parents, family and the handicapped child, thus improving the home environment. In 1970, following the investigation of parental attitudes, child rearing practices, and the training of mentally handicapped children in the home, Dorothy Jeffree, with C. C. Cunningham and colleagues, ran a workshop course for parents of young mentally handicapped children. It was thought that parental feelings '. . . of inadequacy, perplexity, guilt, and even non-acceptance . . .' are, in frequency and intensity '. . . probably less than is sometimes thought'. Direct therapy was therefore not the aim, although it was believed the participative method was likely to have a therapeutic effect upon parental stress.

This early work established that one sort of help, although often sought, was rarely given parents: that is '. . . guidance on how best they can aid their child's cognitive development'. The aim of a current research project is to seek information on how this can best be done, and how this information can effectively be passed on to the professions '. . . who frequently come in contact with parents . . .'; also, to the parents themselves. This research is sponsored jointly by the DHSS and DES (grant £60,800) and the work, under the direction of Peter Mittler, Manchester University, Hester Adrian Research Centre, will be completed in 1977.

1

Working with parents of the newly-born :
Southend Society for Mentally Handicapped Children

Notes were tabled describing a group therapy project for parents of the newly-born. It had been found necessary to begin group therapy with parents at the birth of their child. Groups for parents of older children (2 to 4 years) were much more difficult to run. This is '. . . mainly because parents have often had two years in which to face their problems alone. They had already built up ideas and patterns of life, which precluded the acceptance of the need for group experience'. This suggestion might also apply to disturbed parents of non-handicapped children. Launched in 1970, under the then Deputy Medical Officer of Health, this group therapy project was originally for parents of mixed-age children. The group included parents of an eighteen-month old mongol baby who felt their need was not the same as the parents of older children. They would '. . . prefer to receive guidance as to how to avoid the situation that older parents had found themselves to be in'. This lead to the development of an 0-2 group. A participant suggested that since the aim of helping parents of the newly-born was the avoidance of stress through acceptance, rather than simply presenting a diagnosis, time lapse is valued by some workers, and that this may apply in individual cases: Berg, however, has suggested that the mothers from whom diagnosis is witheld tend to be the most resentful: this suggestion is supported by other studies. It was suggested that parents left to suffer frustration and despair alone were unlikely to provide a good home environment, either for themselves, their family, or their handicapped child.

Local domiciliary services

The main problem was not the built environment of the home, although it was important. Improvement of equipment in the home was not the basic issue. The essential problem was one of communication between the caring professions and the parents. With regard to the Health Visitor Service, there was much room for improvement. Development of specialist health visitors, trained to deal with the handicapped and their families, would be a valuable development in the right direction. Home-helps should also be made more easily available to families with a grievously handicapped dependent. There is also much room for improvement in day-nurseries. Although the child may be given good supportive care, there is often no one to discuss the home management and care of the child with the mother. There is also a lack – or absence – of co-operation between the National Health Service and the education services; for example, in the provision of courses which would aid the parent to enrich the child's home environment – courses such as 'Help to Help the

Child'. In this connection it was also important that education authorities should be prepared to provide peripatetic teachers for the pre-school child, and for the child unable to attend school. Such teachers, properly trained, can make a contribution to the welfare and counselling of parents, and can demonstrate to parents a child's need, and response, to the right kinds of stimulation.

The dangers of stress in the family, for both child and parents were emphasised. Most parents were against their child going into hospital. There was a need for flexible short-stay care, readily available to all parents when they felt they needed it. An example was given of a family, in a small house, with other children who, since they were studying for examinations, found it difficult to make an effective case for 'emergency' short-stay facilities, and yet the home situation could be very difficult indeed. The development by some county authorities, of seaside and country holiday homes was noted. These were designed to provide short-term care relief for old people, battered wives and those, including the handicapped, whose families, from time to time, were in need of this kind of temporary relief. Holiday provisions were one useful supplement to short-stay relief.

During 1974 nine separate holidays have been provided by the NSMHC, four of these for special care cases. Whilst some parents needed persuading to let their child attend holidays of this kind, it is important that this effort be made. There was also a need for active work towards a better understanding by local authorities (both housing and social services), so that families can be made more aware of the help that can be given them in improving the physical structure of the home. An ageing father carried his adult son on his back upstairs to toilet and bathroom; there was no shower or toilet on the ground floor. Whilst washing machines and play equipment can improve a home, it is absurd to consider these aids when more basic housing improvement, for which local authorities are responsible, remains neglected. The rights of parents to them are not yet clearly understood. Research undertaken before the Seebohm reorganisation showed that families saw the Mental Health Welfare Officer (a) as central to satisfying their needs, (b) that he also saw this as his own role and (c) that with his disappearance, the new Director of Social Services would face a hiatus that '. . . will demand ingenuity to solve'. But the same project also demonstrated why feedback was unlikely; that is, why when research of this kind is available from most information departments, notice may not be taken of it.

3

The statutory services

The Department of Education and Science

Schools for the ESN (S). Recent developments in bridging the gap between school and home were outlined. These developments were aimed at providing a better service to parents through encouraging participation, and in this way enabling parents to improve the home environment. A big parent/teacher association was described at one school which provides (*a*) information, (*b*) speakers for meetings and (*c*) social events, dances and plays that encourage the parents to meet together. For about a year there have been two specialist education social workers; one of these workers serves the ESN(S) school, and also the ESN School. Through the education social worker the parents' needs in respect of housing, social services and health can be co-ordinated. The problem of 'wrestling' for hearing aids, glasses, and the other needs of individual parents and their children, can now be looked after by specialised staff. The education authority provides the services of a psychologist to provide tutorials for the teaching staff, to advise both teachers and parents on management problems, to undertake in special cases home visits, and to advise on special topics – such as behaviour modification. The school admits pre-school children at age 3 years. For parents, and children under age 3, there is an Opportunity Class held regularly which is associated with the school, where parents can meet and discuss problems with teachers, and help prepare the young child for school admission. As these new services develop it appears to become clearer that one of the main stumbling blocks may be the parents themselves; they have difficulty in grouping, co-operating, and seeking benefit from the new services that are now being provided.

The Department of Health and Social Security—The National Health Service

The Centre for Spastic Children (London). The word 'spastic' was really a misnomer – a preferred term would be children with brain damage. This Centre is concerned mainly with children who suffer a dominant physical handicap where development in every sphere is very slow. Their dominant handicap is usually of sufficient strength to mask any ability the children may have. After long term assessment ability is frequently far greater than was first thought. Particularly misleading are the disabilities arising from deafness, sometimes categorised as mental subnormality; often those assumed to have behaviour problems suffer considerable hearing loss. The Centre is classified as a day hospital (60/70 children daily). There is a special care unit for 18 children (6 to 13 years). There is also an opportunity (nursery) group for 12 children and a class for the 5 to 7 years olds (12 children: 1 teacher). Also a small residential hostel, run by a Friends Group, to provide for eight children whose parents are unable to cope. Professional staff include a neurologist, cardiologist, an electro-encephalograph service, (for the detection of abnormal brain-function, through the measurement of electrical pulses), a teacher of the deaf, together with a social worker and occupational therapist. The work of the Centre is directed to helping the child and the parents, and a domiciliary service was begun in 1970. Many infants are members of large families and mothers are unable to sit around for hours awaiting attention. Young infants can receive services at home and there are two physiotherapists who are also domiciliary officers. They can also call upon the services of a speech therapist. Growing children attend normal school, where possible. These children are often sensitive, and prefer not to travel between school and clinic for treatment. This is arranged where possible at the school by the domiciliary officers. The basic aim of the Centre is to see those who attend as people (developing in a limited way), rather than patients in need of hospital services. Whilst the domiciliary services do much to improve the home environment, the apparent 'invasion' of home by too many professional people must be avoided. For this reason, efforts are always made to 'group' visits, and therapists are encouraged to also function as social workers. Of particular importance is the degree to which these visits expose the need for help from housing and social service authorities; the family of six living in one room with a grievously handicapped member; the family with a 5 and 3 year old, living on the tenth floor of a 'high rise' block unable to go out without an adult.

Hospitals for the mentally handicapped. Work with mentally handicapped children in hospitals had shown that there was a great degree of hidden potential awaiting development in many of the children who live in the hospital setting. There was an urgent need for research in this area as the expectations of staff may be too low. Is it possible that the same principle applies to mentally handicapped children who suffer a poor home environment? One attitude that could be taken, to parents, and to the mentally handicapped, was: 'Please help me to help you to help yourselves'. When a child was pulling hard at a parent's hand, you can ask: 'What is he trying to tell us, Mother? – or – 'Are we listening to what he is trying to say?'

The Social Services (Under Directors of Social Service)

A social worker explained to participants the contributions that hospitals for the mentally handicapped make to improving the home environment for the mentally handicapped; children, adults – and their parents.

5

The Ida Darwin Hospital had 8 wards of 30 beds; one of these wards was for the assessment of nursery-age children and two beds in each ward were available for short term care. Considerable effort was made to ensure that this short-stay facility was made available to parents, even if the need was only to permit mother and family to be free to attend special events (birthdays, weddings, christenings). Through the social work department a community nurse, and also senior members of staff, are encouraged to visit the home, with or without a social worker. Referrals came from consultants at the out-patients clinic, and advice can be given to parents in their own homes on management, feeding and similar problems. Parents with infants 0–2 are encouraged to attend the two opportunity classes in the hospital catchment area where they can meet together, benefit from the toy library facilities, and also make contact with hospital staff. There was, however, a need for some kind of 'Universal Aunts Service', to prevent family collapse. Although local authority services were good, (three adult training centres with a fourth opening shortly, and a centre for the severely subnormal adult who is unable to attend a training centre), at certain times, to provide relief in the home, the presence of an understanding person (short-term or longer), was a great need which was not at present met.

Social Services, Winchester. A variety of developments in this area, closely associated with the work of Dr Albert Kushlick, were described. A project had been set up to show how effective special care and training could be for grievously handicapped young adults who were unsuitable for admission to adult training centres. Two years ago two girls, who had finished school, were provided with special care facilities, the staff being $1\frac{1}{2}$ staff to two trainees. Progress had been marvellous. There is now speech; feeding problems are being overcome; double incontinence has been controlled, and sociability increased. There is a waiting list of special care adults and given the outcome of the above demonstration, it is hoped that this work can be extended but it is expensive, and at present further funds are not available. Other developments included the provision of behaviour modification sessions (one full time staff) at a local general hospital: also the use, for short-term care staff, of young graduates, prepared to work one-to-one on individual development programmes. All these developments, in increasing the social acceptance of the mentally handicapped, would tend to reflect in improving the home environment.

Farnborough Hospital. This is a general hospital with specialist units covering a catchment area of the London Borough of Bromley, Bexley and Sevenoaks. There is a clinic where a paediatrician examines all new babies and parents attend with infants up to three years. Over the age of 3 the child may be seen alone, or individual visits be made to the home. All infants thought to have suffered an 'at-risk' birth history are carefully followed-up, and an eye is kept on parents. Diagnostic work is (on occasion) linked with the Spastic Centre (see above). A new unit for cot and chair severely subnormal is being provided. Here the basic work in assisting the parents in the home environment is provided by the social work team attached to the hospital: links are also maintained with the home through local social services departments.

Money matters

Several participants referred to the Attendance Allowance, the Family Fund, and the possible effect of these financial provisions on improving the home environment. A given home may be in receipt of none or all of these benefits, depending upon individual circumstances. All services, in cash and in kind, to which parents are entitled, are listed in 'Parent's Information Bulletin,' current edition published NSMHC. This publication has largely eliminated questions from parents by letters and telephone. In A to Z order the answers given cover the categories of entitlement – in cash and in kind – now available to parents. Cash entitlements include social security supplementary benefits in addition to which, in specific cases, there is the attendance allowance (a statutory provision) and the benefits of the Family Fund (semi-statutory, funded by government capital, with income applied by a non-statutory body). In addition to these 'cash and kind' provisions, there are also the services and supplies available through social services departments and the National Health Service. A pilot project used 'Parent's Voice' the Journal of the NSMHC to circulate a questionnaire on (a) the use made by parents of official services and (b) the effect a mentally handicapped child has upon the life of the family, including the financial consequences. Although many parents said they had no financial problems, a number mentioned particular expenses. The pilot sample was small and heavily biased (middle-class parents). Four hundred questionnaires were sent, ninety-seven returned completed and thirty-five were returned from non-parent readers. Little is known of the fairness with which this system (from all to nothing) operates, or the extent to which, in specific cases, money matters.

The Attendance Allowance. There are no official figures which show how recipients spend this Allowance. From the administrative point of view (unlike the Family Fund) the way the allowance is spent is not relevant. But it was clear that this information would be of use to those concerned with the improvement of the home environment for the handicapped. The following material from two ongoing research projects was reported to the Session:—

Southampton Survey. This survey relates to one South Coast town and may not be typical. Just over 1,000 people were interviewed and of these 75 were receiving attendance allowance, a fairly small sample. On general financial issues, nearly 80% of the 75 said that they found it easier to manage now that they had the allowance. In detail, only 8% of the beneficiaries in fact spent the allowance on paying for help; 16% spent it on fuel bills and extra heating; 15% on extra or special clothes; 28% on a miscellany of items including extra food, holidays, washing machines, car expenses, house decorations, extra mortgage after alterations due to illness, and relieving husband of need to work overtime. Of the rest 21% said there was nothing and 12% gave no answer.

York Survey. This was postal and nationwide but restricted to children. There were 245 questionnaires issued and the question relating to the spending of attendance allowance contained 9 items. Most people chose more than one item of expenditure and in fact 72% chose 2 to 4 items. There was no significant difference between higher and lower rate allowance but there was a relationship between disability and the type of expenditure e.g. incontinence and bedding. The main items were:

Clothing and shoes	75%
Bedding	47%
Transport	46%
Different things each week	43%

The survey included questions also about special food, paying off bills and debts, new things on HP, saving for holidays, home helps and child minders. Additionally 56 people mentioned other things including items which ought to be available from the local authorities ranging from disposable nappies to adaption of the home. In these cases people were ignorant as to what the LA could provide or were not satisfied with the quality of what was on offer. Other items included also life insurance, savings for the child, and laundry costs including launderette, hot water, and soap. There was also some evidence of people feeling under pressure to buy toys and other means of recreation.

Why doctors? With regard to the above research a participant asked why the Attendance Allowance Board used doctors and not social workers for assessment. The reason was that there were not enough social workers to go around: the Board welcomes supplementary reports from social workers. The question was asked whether doctors are the best people to test social handicaps. It was suggested that doctors should use their medical knowledge plus common sense.

The Family Fund. This Fund is anxious to consider new and unusual ways of helping families with children who are severely handicapped. It is often found on visiting the home that the real need of a family can only be met by help from the social services or housing departments: much work is concerned with alerting the authorities to their duties (having a 'fight' with them on behalf of the parents). An example was given of a Methodist Minister who was told by a social worker: 'Look where you live! You cannot expect help from the Family Fund!' This situation arose because of lack of training, and understanding, of the special problems of the handicapped.

The non-statutory services

Improving the built environment

Centre on Environment for the Handicapped. Supported by the DHSS, the Spastics Society and the King's Fund, this organisation comprises two staff and two part-time consultants. The Centre provides advisory services on all aspects of building for handicapped people. This includes advice on adaption of homes and kitchens and the Centre organises a monthly Seminar on topics of special interest to the handicapped – including the mentally handicapped. An exhibition has been recently mounted and is likely to be available for display in areas where there is a demand for information in respect of improving the physical environment of the home.

Extending home life: play and leisure

Play. The work of the Toy Libraries Association was described; this Association caters for the special needs of the handicapped: for example, in the case of the mentally handicapped, the fact that physical size outgrows mental age: the need to cater for a two-year old child with the strength of a grown-up person. Appropriate toys can add to the enjoyment of the whole family and thus enrich the home. A good toy library can become a centre for discussion between parents, where they can exchange information. When children 'grow-out' of toys, the toys can be changed. Toys can cover a wide spectrum of need – from therapy to fun.

Leisure. *Gatepost** the Newsletter of the National Federation of Gateway Clubs was tabled. Gateway's contribution to improving the home environ-

---

* Obtainable from Gateway Office, Pembridge Hall, Pembridge Square, London W2 4EP

ment is expanding as the value of meaningful leisure-time programmes for the mentally handicapped is recognised. To some parents the regular meeting of the Gateway Club, or the annual club holiday, provides them with an opportunity to relax and have some time to themselves in the knowledge that their child is happy and cared for in the sympathetic environment of the club. The child invariably returns home, having enjoyed the evening, ready to relate the happenings of the last few hours. In an increasing number of clubs there is the facility for parents who bring their child to the club to meet with other parents and discuss matters, or problems of mutual interest, listen to a guest speaker, or just relax. The introduction of the Gateway Award Scheme is encouraging greater participation on the part of the parent in the various stages of the Scheme. Learning to care for self and possessions is all part of the 'Design for Living' section. A period of three months effort is required in the Hobby section and the member will choose an activity of particular interest to work on both at home and in the club. Parental co-operation greatly assists.

Improving links with home/community/hospital/and special services

Centre for the Mentally Handicapped. The aims of this new project – set up to provide new kinds of supportive services to the mentally handicapped, mainly in the Tower Hamlets, City and Hackney areas were outlined. The Centre's age range will be unlimited. Projects will involve a One-to-One (hyperactive), Saturdays (12 children plus 12 volunteers); a Baby-Sitting Project (for parents); a child accompanying service, for children whose parents do not find it easy to take them out on tubes and buses; a pre-Gateway 11–14 year old club; a 'ten hour day out' for the hospitalised or institutionalised, with collection and delivery from hospitals by volunteers and (specifically) the use of public transport. There will also be an information and counselling service, run both within the Centre, and also projected into the homes of those who cannot visit. There will also be one-to-one projects organised inside hospitals (with the non-communicating and non-ambulant): also projects for those over 16 in the community who are unsuitable for training centres. It is hoped that this down-to-earth approach to helping the mentally handicapped will not only aid in improving the home environment, through relieving stress and increasing enjoyment, but that it will also become a model to be followed elsewhere, where similar services are needed.

Local welfare services project. In 1973 the number of local societies affilliated to the NSMHC with voluntary welfare visitors numbered 163. Now there are over 400 local societies in England, Wales and Northern

Ireland. The aim of the present scheme, under the direction of James Ross, previously Regional Officer, NSMHC South-East Region, is to provide an 'organised framework of support' for the development of these services; to provide guide-lines for the selection and appointment of visitors and to provide a programme of information and training, both regionally and nationally. A Memorandum sets out the functions of a local welfare visitor and outlines the content of the Regional Courses which will be provided. One of the many aims of the new local welfare service was to bring to the attention of all parents the many services which are now available to them: for example, the services that were the subject of this current Information Exchange.

Helping where help is not understood. The special problems of the underprivileged. The special problems that arise in areas of gross social change were described in relation to the work of the Lady-wood Family Centre, Birmingham. The area served by this Family Centre is mainly in the process of being knocked down and re-built. It is an area where houses are 'vandalised' and over-run with rats: where the Housing Department is systematically running down and re-building: where there are insecure tenants, or those who do not belong to the place they live in – Irish, immigrant. There is often no effective male member, and no extended family (aunts, grandmothers). Under these conditions it is more a question of 'assisting survival' than 'improving the home environment'. The Centre provides for a group of 74 under-fives. There are a number of mentally handicapped children, and there are about 90 admissions a year. An effort is made, in addition to providing for the children, to work with the parents in maintaining a home-life. But of the 74 children, 30 come from one parent families, 15 from families suffering marital stress, 30 have severe family problems, 20 homes are dirty and of poor condition, 12 parents and/or children suffer severe handicap, and 9 are over-large in family size. (This adds up to more than 74. Frequently two or three conditions apply to one family). About 50% of cases are referred by the local authority: the rest make use of the Centre direct. Those that most need help are not necessarily the ones that get it. The referral may be due to a special crisis: many of the children, if not provided for by the Centre, would certainly require residential care. But if day care was cheaper than residential care, why was there not more money available? The Centre had on tap a multi-disciplinary service of professions: health visitors, general practitioners, hospital services, educational psychologists, speech therapists, the dental services and so on: but in a voluntary organisation there is just not the staff to do the co-ordinating. There are the failed appointments and the necessity to collect and deliver by transport. From the point of view of helping

11

improve the home, the main problem that requires attack is a lack of effective mothering. The mothers do care, they do know, but there is invariably a conflict between (a) the needs of the children and (b) the desires of the parents. In these circumstances and with most parents lacking in maturity there is considerable psychiatric disorder. With a constant struggle to pay off rent arrears, catch up with credit in the shops, and the under valuation of themselves as women on the marriage market, these mothers don't need to be preached at – they need organising – and above all – they need respecting. Work with these parents involves (a) prevention (the discovery that children are being left unattended) (b) stand by/await crisis (c) move in/stay in (d) provide consistency and reliability (e) await self-help response. For the mothers their main wish is that they should be treated like women. The stages of this process are (a) apathy (b) out of apathy into aggression (c) criticism (what are you doing about it) (d) demands for help (e) attempts to do something for self. At a Wednesday afternoon 'Parent Group' they do what they want to do. Most of them desire most of all to fill in the adolescent experiences they have missed out: go swimming; play table tennis; or they go in for short-term ego-boosting: men; drink; drugs; tobacco. For them mothering can have no meaning: to their children they still have nothing yet to give.

Spreading professional knowledge. It was suggested that the knowledge of a small number of professionals needs to be spread as widely as possible. Recent projects for parents working with professional people at Nottingham University were described, and also the work of 'Kith and Kids'.

Realistic expectations. It was also suggested that voluntary organisations should help to bring parents and professionals together. Parents can have over-high expectations. Parents compare their child with non-handicapped children of the same chronological age: but even mental age can only be an approximation: a child's motor, language and social developments may all be at different stages. A wider meaning must be given to the word 'education'.

Parent/Teacher co-operation

The Session Editor had suggested that the parents were an important part of the home environment. This suggestion was touched on in discussion by a number of participants: it was also suggested that improvements, if made, were likely to be affected by them. Mrs Alison Stallibrass introduced a book she had published recently on the topic of children's play and development. Although her book was concerned with apparently non-handicapped children Mrs Stallibrass said that it was likely that normal child development was a base against which work on special handicaps can proceed. She mentioned the idea of a new-born baby kept in solitary confinement in a pitch dark, sound-proof room: the possible range of environments for a child were so great (from bad to good) that even a child born normal could be handicapped by a negative environment. She gave as example – jumping. She said that jumping, in a young child, is a natural function of the human body. It is one of the powers a small child finds the need to nourish through appropriate and timely exercise. If starved of this exercise it will fail to grow: the child will be handicapped. This, Mrs Stallibrass said, was dependent upon the opportunities given to the child to jump (be it home/school or any other environment). This in turn depends upon adult attitudes (parents/teachers) to the information which is available on how children grow, and what they need to help them to grow. Mrs Stallibrass had worked at the Peckham Experiment. The aim of this was to seek information on the behaviour of healthy people in an environment made by them. The aim was also to see if use of this information could be encouraged in 'man-made' urban environments. At the time (1939–1945) when nations were directly confronted with the consequences of the environments they were making, the Peckham Experiment won world-wide acclaim. Since the war the idea became more popular and was applied to the play and development of children.

Physical activity. The Session Editor said that every opportunity must be given to the handicapped child (who may lack motivation) to engage in physical activity. This means providing the right environment. Motor skills form an important part of a child's early play and are also essential to his cognitive development. Experience in this area is important for symbolic development in general, including language development.

Motivation. It was noted that, in a recent book written by Dr Doman it was suggested that it is success that creates motivation: failure destroys it. To teach a child to succeed, however minimally, is to teach it motivation. None of us choose what we fail at, however good it may be for us morally: we try to repeat our successes. Dr Doman discusses in this book the controversy his work has aroused in the professions concerned with the mentally handicapped child. This may be due to his central suggestion – that functions can determine structure: that is, unless you use a thing, you will never know whether you can get better at using it: or as Dr Doman puts it – 'weight lifters have huge muscles because they lift weights – they do not lift weights because they have huge muscles!'

Baselines. Two books, both concerned with the home training of retarded young people were discussed and a home-teacher, who had worked with one of the retarded persons, referred in particular to the need for seeking a 'base-line', and the importance of this, in co-operative work between parent, teacher and pupil. The Session Editor outlined to non-teaching participants the particular value of baselines. It is essential when working with handicapped children to observe them: that is, to see them as they are, and not as they ought to be. It is of little use saying that a child can read at $7\frac{1}{2}$ years. What is vital is the careful observation of which words he can, and which words he cannot read. You do not want to teach what a child already knows; you must not teach beyond what he is ready to learn. Any programme, be it teaching, or behaviour modification, must begin without pre-conceived ideas; that is, with accurate observation. Before we start, we need a baseline to measure progress and assess the effectiveness of our teaching. Mother says she is worried: Harold is always spitting on the window! But you say 'Always? How many times does Harold do it? A hundred times a day?' You ask mother to count how many times Harold does it; also when he does it. Then perhaps mother will find out that Harold only spits on the window when he is bored! Perhaps for ten years Harold has done nothing, except teach himself how to spit on the window, and because it is far harder to teach a child to un-learn, rather than teaching a child to learn, mother must be told it will take a long time. But mother will also have learned: she will have learned the value of using observations, and also the value of using baselines, in her co-operation with teacher.

Unlearning. A participant questioned the Session Editor on the point of 'unlearning'. She said that her own child de-educates very quickly indeed. She gave as example her own programme of toilet training which led to her child being clean. After a short stay in hospital this training is completely lost, and she has to start again. Points similar to this arose during the Session, which indicated that participants would have liked to take up these separate topics, in depth, and call on the professional wisdom of the Session Editor for guidance. Time at a one-day Session was clearly not available for this. The demand did demonstrate the need for education and training organisations to take this matter up, so that the necessary services could be provided.

Home aids for parent/teacher. The Director of Publications (NSMHC) submitted the following note for the consideration of participants:
'The National Society has been for some time aware of the need of a very simple method of progress assessment for very young children. Having regard to the fact that the person most likely to be in intimate contact with the child from birth to infant school age is the mother, and that the mother will be fully engaged with other household duties em-

bracing the whole family, it is realised that she will have very little time for reading. It is therefore essential that any programme designed for the child from birth must be capable of performance within the normal routine of family life and not place undue strain on the programme of family life for the other members. Many activities thought of as instinctive to any mother, e.g. the loving, stroking and close contact with the child, the speaking to him and the rocking movements made whilst handling him, are not instinctive and have in fact to be taught. These stimulating activities are essential for all children but doubly so for a handicapped child. It is important that the mother should be given some guidance on the amount of time she should spend in any stimulating activity as over-enthusiastic application of simple principles may exhaust both child and mother. A handicapped child, especially a child who is mentally handicapped, will not initiate the normal development responses at the expected chronological age and will require stimulation to achieve them. A stimulation chart from the U.S.A. produced by an inter-disciplinary team of four workers attempts to give guidance to the mother of a normal baby from birth to 5 years and gives very simple directions to enable the mother to use her routine of child care – feeding, bathing, moving the child – as periods for specific stimulation. This guide is a very useful starting point. There is an activity sheet to enable the parent to record the successful accomplishment of the activities suggested and also to record whether the child responded to the activity or not. For parents who appreciate a systematic approach to loving and mothering and for parents whose child has a greater need of a systematic approach to stimulation, the use of a simple chart of this kind is valuable. The National Society would like to design a chart of special value to the parents of mentally handicapped children and would appreciate any suggestions which would enable such a chart to be useful. The following criteria are necessary:

1. The age of the child must be clearly stated and at the younger level broken down into three-month periods.
2. The upper and lower levels of time suggested for each activity should be given as a guide. For example, it is not sufficient to say 'Continue an activity for about 15 minutes'. It is better to say 'The activity should be persevered with for at least 10 minutes and should not be continued beyond 20 minutes'. This will avoid an anxious mother starting and stopping too many different activities in a short space of time, or persevering to fatigue point with an activity which is unsuccessful with the child.
3. The activity must be clearly described in very simple language. For example, it is not sufficient to say 'Let a child explore the

toy with his mouth' without the caution that no child should be left for one moment with a toy in his mouth.

4. Be careful to make it clear that the chronological age of the child is not necessarily the same as his mental age and that parents commencing an activity programme with an unresponsive child aged, for example, two years, may achieve success if they commence with activities designed for a much younger child.

5. It should be emphasized that what has been referrred to as 'activity' in many cases is what is usually regarded as play and the element of fun and pleasure therefore must never be forgotten in designing an instructional programme of this kind.

6. Whatever programme is designed it must be capable of being reproduced by the cheapest possible method of production compatible with clarity of presentation.

Those who have had experience of activity programmes which fit the foregoing criteria for mentally retarded children are asked to communicate with us.'

Parents in the environment

The Session Editor, during the morning Session, said she hoped that, if parents could be worked with when their children were at an earlier age, fewer of these children would be placed in residential care. Opening the afternoon session Miss Jeffree pointed out some of the dangers of the multi-disciplinary approach. Parents sometimes received conflicting advice from specialists working on different lines. To resolve these difficulties members of a team had, on occasion, to be willing to be flexible within their own discipline in order to become members of an integrated team. Parents themselves should also be accepted as equal partners in this team. Ten years of research into mental handicap had taught Miss Jeffree how relatively little we know as yet of the early development of the mentally handicapped child. Many of the parents we meet know more about the bringing up of the mentally handicapped child in the home than we do. We should beware of expertise: our contribution may not be wanted. If parents are prepared to meet us, it is their expertise we should seek. We should try and find out why what they are doing is excellent. Miss Jeffree drew attention to the limits of professionalism in the upbringing of any young child. Research has shown that in the years 0–5 (the vital years in the development of any child) parents are usually more effective than highly qualified and caring staff in residential establishments. At this age the maximum development takes place in the home with caring parents; even the complex acquisition of language does not normally require the services of a professional; this too, is best learnt in the home. However, in the rare event of the normal parent/child relationship failing to lead to language development then professional aid may be needed. Anyone can be a parent and we can only be effective when we accept them as they are. Our contribution is not to bring about a radical change, but, in the light of our specialised knowledge, to increase confidence by explaining the rationale of what they are attempting. We may add form and substance to what the parents are attempting and help them to see the situation with greater objectivity and so bring about a more positive approach. It was difficult not to have lots of 'bright ideas'. But Miss Jeffree said that she had learned to hold on to them: at least until the second visit or the visit after that! If you are a parent you are in a key position to seek your own solutions: these will be better than any imposed by others, they will 'fit' the family circumstances. We have continually to be asking ourselves the question 'What is our aim?' It is not, of course, to display our specialised knowledge. Personal experience is more important than dependence upon the literature especially where parents are concerned. By the time something is printed it may be out of date and many stereotyped ideas can become perpetuated.

Like other people. In response to a question Miss Jeffree said she thought that parents ought to be seen as members of the professional team. But a participant, as the Session concluded, and with regard to the provision of special services, special visitors and the aids that had been discussed for improving the home environment, said that, with regard to her own child and family, she would like either the money to pay for these, or would like them as normal services; the same as others get, through their own local channels. She did not want her front-door to stick out. She wanted it to look like other peoples.

Multi-disciplinary dangers. With regard to the suggestion that the multi-disciplinary approach had its dangers, these could be of many different kinds; it was necessary to distinguish between them. When these teams meet in conference together many of the professions are not trained to understand that each of us as individuals have many sides to ourselves, and many roles to play. 'The social worker will usually be aware of these many sides of us since she (or he) will have been trained consciously to switch to each according to activity (say wife, mother, social worker, administrator, etc.). The other members of the multi-disciplinary team may not have been taught to do this. Therefore, those of the team representing the professional caring skills may simply be speaking as emotive persons, and not limiting themselves to their own professional discipline.' It is because a social worker may be more fully aware in the use of these skills that they may well become the best link between the multiple disciplines (education, medicine, pscyhology, etc.) and the parents themselves. Of the many roles that professionals play there is that of being 'an authority'. For the social worker this charisma is projected by the client on to us – it is not the other way around. The well trained professional will use this 'projection' as just one more tool for the job in the individual case (every 'case' is specific). The parents who project authority on to you, usually do so because they need it (at the beginning). If parents do not project it, then no pretence should be made of having it: clearly this would offend them. Unless the basis for all work with a client is that of one human being to another, each seeking to recover wholeness, then those without this capacity should not choose this kind of career.

The Session Editor writes:

There can be no doubt that improving the home environment is still a pressing need today notwithstanding the expansion of available services (both statutory and voluntary) and the changing social attitude towards mental handicap. This information exchange has highlighted some of the areas in which improvement could be brought about.

Improvement will continue to be uneven and fail to reach many homes so long as the channels of communication are inadequate. Many participants referred to this.

Much concern was expressed on the way in which parents are told of their child's handicap and its implications. Many parents had not been told of the handicap early enough and had not had the implications explained to them. Some parents were completely unaware of the nature of their child's handicap. Although there are differences of opinion as to when and how parents should be told, most parents agree that the present system is far from satisfactory.

Many participants agreed that parents remained unaware of the help available to them. No adequate machinery has yet been devised to enable parents to know where they can get help as soon as they know that their child is handicapped.

Many references were made to attempts to get co-operation between parents and professionals; also the need to provide peripatetic teachers for the pre-school child. Many ways of co-operation between parents and schools can be fostered, and co-operation between parents and hospitals for the mentally handicapped can help the home situation. It became apparent that this co-operation is actively fostered in some places but is by no means universal.

At present many families collapse for lack of an understanding person to play a supportive role. This is an area in which other parents or para-professionals would be recruited. As a participant described it, we could do with a 'Universal Aunts' service.

An extension of workshops for parents, which would give them some expertise in teaching their children and dealing with behaviour problems would not only directly benefit the children's development but also improve the home environment by enabling parents to get more enjoyment from their children.

The problem of inadequate parents and one parent families living in appalling conditions is still rife. Often mental and physical handicap is also present. The description of the work of the Ladywood Family Centre made us aware of personal qualities needed by anybody attempting to make any impact on this kind of home environment. This was summed up by the saying: 'these mothers don't need to be preached at – they need organising – and above all – they need respecting'. Hopefully the way ahead will bring many other people with this positive attitude to work in this field.

It became apparent that many families were unaware of the sources of financial and practical assistance, or of their statutory rights. Voluntary organisations and particularly the National Society for Mentally Handicapped Children have done much to improve this situation for their members, but there remain many families who are unaware of the existence of such a society. In these days of mass media it should surely be possible to improve this situation.

It became apparent that some local authorities interpret their obligations as regards housing and help from the social services much more liberally than others. Often there is little understanding of the problems facing the families of the mentally handicapped. Parents themselves were often unable to obtain the help to which they were entitled. We heard how a caseworker for the Family Fund could often alert local authorities to their duties in cases where parents had been unsuccessful.

It is still not known the extent to which financial assistance alone can improve the home environment. However, it is now generally recognized that such financial assistance is needed. Government recognition of this need is a great step forward. This service is having teething troubles and attention was drawn to cases in which the system for administering allowances has left much to be desired. The extension of the Family Fund gives hope for further improvement of the home environment.

Professionals are becoming increasingly aware that there is often inadequate communication between those who come into contact with a family. We heard of many instances where there was excellent co-operation between doctors, social workers, health visitors, psychologists and teachers, who all worked as members of a team. However, we cannot afford to be complacent nor assume that this is universal. The idea that parents themselves can become part of the multi-disciplinary team is not accepted by some professionals but is gaining ground.

In the grim struggle to cope with problems of existence the importance of recreation and fun can often be forgotten. In their different ways the activities of toy libraries and Gateway Clubs are alerting us to this aspect of improving the home environment. Again we find these amenities being used much more in some areas than in others; possibly we should start to examine how best to involve the parents.

Having highlighted some of the areas of concern and heard many pioneer ventures described, we can, I think, start planning the way ahead without undue pessimism or undue optimism either.

If we are to plan for the future we need to be clear headed and realistic about the present situation. Today's proceedings have shown us that there is a wind of change blowing – however this wind of change is long overdue and blows more strongly in some parts of the country than in others.

Again, although it is impressive and heartwarming to hear what is being done to improve the home environment we should put this in the context of all possible improvements which still remain to be done.

Dorothy Jeffree

Individual contributions are identified by page and line number on the List of Participants. References are identified by page and line, in the same way.

Participants Lists give the name, address, telephone number and post held at the time the contribution was made.

LIST OF PARTICIPANTS

SESSION EDITOR:
MISS D. M. JEFFREE, M.Ed.
Research Fellow & Project Director,
Hester Adrian Research Centre,
Manchester University,
Manchester M13 9PL.
Telephone: 061-273 3333

PARTICIPANTS

	page	*lines*

HOBBS, SISTER MARGARET   Superintendent, Ladywood Family   11–12   12–21
Centre, 2/4 Guild Close, Ladywood, Birmingham 16
Telephone: 021-454 8326

JAMES, B. G.   Secretary, Attendance Allowance Board, Room 12A,   7–9   34– 3
Ingram House, 13/15 John Adam Street, London WC2M 6HD
Telephone: 01-217 3000

JOLLY, MRS. C.   Social Worker, London Borough of Westminster,   17–18   30–13
71 Queensway, London W2 4QH
Telephone: 01-727 6464

KING, V.   Charge Nurse, Queen Mary's Hospital for Children,   5   27–33
Carshalton, Surrey SM5 4NR
Telephone: 01-643 3300

McCARTHY, MISS J. R.   Regional Officer, East Midlands Region,   2–3   24–32
NSMHC, 28a Regent Street, Nottingham NG1 5BQ
Telephone: Nottingham 42129

MANNING, MISS J.   Publicity Assistant, NSMHC, Pembridge Hall,
17 Pembridge Square, London W2 4EP
Telephone: 01-229 8941

MORLAND, MRS. L.   Director, Toy Libraries Association, Toynbee   9   24–32
Hall, 28 Commercial Street, London E1 6LS   12   22–26
Telephone: 01-247 1497

NEWTON, MRS. J.   Assistant, Local Welfare Services (Field Studies),
NSMHC, Pembridge Hall, 17 Pembridge Square, London W2 4EP
Telephone: 01-229 8941

PRESTON, REV. GEOFFREY O. P.   Holy Priory, Leicester
Telephone: Leicester 28846

RUST, MRS. J.   Secretary, Centre on Environment for the   9   14–23
Handicapped, 24 Nutford Place, London W1
Telephone: 01-262 2641   Ext: 25

SHENNAN, MRS. V.   Director of Publications, NSMHC, Pembridge   14–16   35–18
Hall, 17 Pembridge Square, London W2 4EP
Telephone: 01-229 8941

SOUTHWOOD, MISS V. J., BSC, SRN, HV   Project Officer, Disabled
Living Foundation, 346 Kensington High Street, London W14 8NS
Telephone: 01-602 2491

STALLIBRASS, MRS. A.   Author, Turkey Island Corner, East   12–13   34–15
Harting, Petersfield, Hampshire
Telephone: Harting 220

SUTTON, MRS. F.   Welfare Secretary, Bromley Society for Mentally   14   24–34
Handicapped Children, 61 Birkbeck Road, Beckenham, Kent   17   21–29
Telephone: 01-778 5825

WOOD, MISS F. B.   Head Teacher, John F. Kennedy School,   4   1–25
Pitchford Street, Stratford, London E15
Telephone: 01-534 8544

WYMAN, MISS R.   Director, Centre for the Mentally Handicapped,   10   18–36
Toynbee Hall, 28 Commercial Street, London E1 6LS.
Telephone: 01-247 4876

REFERENCES

	page	lines

CUNNINGHAM, C. C. and JEFFREE, D. M. 'Working with parents' (1971) NSMHC North West Region. NSMHC. — page 1, lines 15

JEFFREE, D. M. and McCONKEY, R. 'Parental involvement in facilitating the development of young mentally handicapped children' (1974) Manchester University. — page 1, lines 25

HEWETT, S. and NEWSON J. and E. 'The family and the handicapped child' (1970) George Allen and Unwin. — page 2, lines 8

SOUTHEND SOCIETY FOR MENTALLY HANDICAPPED CHILDREN: 'Notes on the running of group therapy for parents of mentally handicapped children' (1973) NSMHC. — page 2, lines 1

BERG, J. M., GILERDALE, S. and WAY, J. 'On telling parents of a diagnosis of mongolism' (1969) British Journal of Psychiatry. 115, 11951/6. — page 2, lines 21

REVANS, R. W. and BAQUER, A. 'I thought they were supposed to be doing that' (1972) Hospital Centre, London. — page 3, lines 39

LLOYD-BOSTOCK, S. (Unpublished notes) The Centre for Socio-Legal Studies, Wolfson College, Oxford. — page 7, lines 34

JOLLY, C. 'The Family Fund: could it help your child' (September 1974) 'Parent's Voice,: The Journal of the NSMHC. — page 9, lines 5

NOTTINGHAM UNIVERSITY: Memorandum. NUTL/4 (1974) on the Nottingham University Toy Library, run in conjunction with a research project 'Play in the remediation of handicap' (Lists information sheets and audio tapes available). — page 9, lines 32

NSMHC: 'Local Welfare Services in the NSMHC' Memorandum (March 1974) NSMHC. — page 11, lines 8

STALLIBRASS, A. 'The self-respecting child: a study of children's play and development' (1974) Thames and Hudson. — page 12, lines 39

PEARSE, I. H. and CROCKER, C. H. 'The Peckham experiment' (1943) George Allen and Unwin, London. — page 13, lines 16

SCOTT WILLIAMSON, G. and PEARSE, I. H. 'Science, synthesis and sanity' (1965) Collins, London. — page 13, lines 16

SHERIDAN, M. D. 'The developmental progress of infants and young children' (1968) Department of Health and Social Security. HMSO. — page 13, lines 3

DOMAN, G. 'What to do about your brain injured child' (1974) Jonathan Cape. — page 13, lines 40

WILKS, J. and E. 'Bernard': bringing up our mongol son' (1974) Routledge and Kegan Paul. — page 13, lines 42

BROWN, R. 'One of seven is special: home training of a retarded child' (1974) NSMHC. — page 13, lines 42

STEVENS, M. 'Observing children who are severely subnormal: an approach to their education' (1968) Edward Arnold, London Reprint 1971. — page 14, lines 6

KRAJICEC, M. (and associates) 'Stimulation activity guide for children from birth to 5 years' (1974) University of Colorado Medical Centre, U.S.A. — page 15, lines 26

MIXING AND GROUPING

Session Editor: D A Purrett
City of Oxford Social Services Department

Mixing and grouping for training and sheltered work

Training (In Local Authority Adult Training Centres: under Directors of Social Service)

Mixing. Information was provided on the development of the Ashford Training Centre, where there is some mixing of the mentally ill and mentally handicapped. Several participants from adult training centres raised the need for information sources, to which reference might be made, on the mixing of the mentally handicapped and other kinds of disability. This with particular regard to the proper use of the space and accommodation, the use of appropriate staff, and the possible need for specially trained staff.

Need to define role of adult training centres. A training centre Manager suggested there was a pressing need for an Information Session on: 'The Role of the Adult Training Centre.' The Secretary explained that Information Sessions were limited to specific topics. A seminar, or course, to define the aims of adult training, might be more appropriate. This matter would be referred, for advice, to the Hon. Advisor to the Information Series (Dr Guy Wigley).[1]

Training: In residential training establishments

Although most participants from hospitals were making some progress in the mixing of sexes, it was suggested that there were many hospitals, not represented at the Session, where such attempts at mixing were strictly limited. A written contribution had therefore been asked for from the Director of a NSMHC Residential Project, at Dilston Hall in Northumberland. It should be noted that this information refers to young men and women who have had the benefit, in general, of an upbringing in the

[1] *Since this Information Exchange a Conference has been held: see Reference List.*

community. They are likely therefore to be more amenable to the encouragement (by the staff) of self-regulation: that is, as compared to those who for most of their lives have been exposed to segregation and institutionalisation.

'Mixing of the sexes in residential establishments. From the outset it must be understood that you cannot legislate for, at best, love and affection and at worst basic 'animal instincts'. If the mentally handicapped of both sexes are to live side by side then the resultant problems must be faced and dealt with realistically. If those responsible are fearful of these problems and are unwilling to mix the sexes then they must be prepared to face different and even much more unpleasant difficulties. Accepting that sexual intercourse will often result from boys and girls and men and women living together it seems to me sensible, firstly to accept that pregnancies in mentally handicapped females is inadvisable and secondly, since intercourse cannot be avoided, reasonable to arrange for problem women and girls to receive the contraceptive pill. This is not to be seen as an excuse to permit sexual orgies. Far from it. Dignified supervision is, of course, necessary but this course of action does, at least, prevent procreation where this is unwise.

I have a very philosophical attitude to this problem as might be suggested by the foregoing. Promiscuity among the type of girls resident at Dilston Hall is fairly common. These ESN youngsters are either down right sex mad or sexually naive but if friendship between the sexes is not to be allowed here, then in terms of social training we shall fail. I cannot speak with much authority for hospital situations but it seems to me that much the same rules apply. Given a situation where sleeping quarters are adequately separated then day time mixing in a single unit is, I feel, a good thing. I also believe that 'pairing' has a therapeutic effect on many sub-normals. At Dilston, I insist on those youngsters of the opposite sex who wish to pair off coming to ask me officially. I then spell out to them the fact that, firstly, they are not at Dilston Hall to find girl friends and boy friends but since 'courting' is part of growing up I have no objection to them being friendly with one or two exceptions to their behaviour. I make it quite clear to them for instance that I do not permit public petting because this is an embarrassment to other people and should not be indulged in and I also make it clear to the boy that the girl is not his 'property'. I also warn the girl of the outcome of 'offering her services', to the boy. This conversation is usually quite frank and carried out without embarrassment and leaves the young people in no doubt as to what is expected of them in terms of behaviour. Some of the ideas these youngsters have regarding sexual matters are hilarious in the extreme and it is quite often necessary to straighten them out in these

26

matters from the outset. This practice seems to have eliminated problems previously experienced in respect of arguments among the boys and girls as to who is 'going' with whom and apart from the occasional bawling out by me for public 'necking' in the Television Room our problems in respect of mixing have been reduced to negligible proportions.

To try and stop 'pairing' is to bang one's head against a brick wall. To allow it with some control and supervision makes not only for a quieter life when working in a residential situation with the mentally handicapped but also often helps the resident patient or trainee to a fuller existence. One happy marriage has resulted from our attitude to this aspect of care and training!

G. Franklin Gray Director, Dilston Hall'

Sheltered Work

Provisions in local authority areas. Several participants from adult training centres informed the Session that they now had numbers of trained mentally handicapped awaiting placement in sheltered work. Information was required on the kinds of provision that could be made for them.

Mixing and grouping children

Mixing handicapped children with non-handicapped children

Ebley House. Information was provided on Ebley House, a project for grouping together – in one mix – both handicapped and non-handicapped children. The residential home, which caters for 16 children is associated with a Nursery School (under the local education authority) which some of the resident children attend: other children attend daily at local schools for normal children or, as appropriate, at special schools. Whilst the handicapped children, including the mentally handicapped, benefit greatly from mixing with the normal children, it is also true to say that the normal children sometimes imitate the handicapped; their progress might be affected by this. The handicapped children took up a very great deal of staff time, to the disadvantage of the normal children. The normal children did not like this. This point is carefully being looked at, and could possibly be put right by a proper distribution of staff; the main problem, however, was the lack of availability of suitable staff with a vocation and training for the sort of work (i.e. work with both handicapped and normal children). A number of participants saw this as a very go-ahead scheme and suggested that if the ratio of normal to handicapped children (which is at present eight to eight) was more in line with their normal distribution in the community (say one to ten for mild and major handicaps) some of these problems might disappear. Reference was made to 'a child is a child' – not a bundle of handicaps – and to Professor Dybwad's well known phrase; 'Label the service, not the child.'

In playgroups

It was suggested that the information sought might be available from the mixing and grouping experience available from pre-school playgroups. In the absence of playgroup participants the available literature was summarized. This literature included publications on the kind of organisation required in playgroups, and the handicaps dealt with; also, a description of an Opportunity Class begun in 1966 which provides 'a nursery class for any handicapped child from birth to seven years, an opportunity for normal children to play together, and a meeting for mothers, held at the same time and place, yet apart, from their children.'

Acceptance and attitudes. The extent to which public attitudes, as reflected by a nursery supervisor, may govern the acceptance or rejection of a handicapped child in an ordinary playgroup is stated by Margaret Crozier (NSMHC Senior Advisory and Counselling Officer). The following key paragraph is taken from a PPA Journal, now out of print.

'It is clearly no good wishing to send a child to a nursery where the supervisor is not interested in him or feels unable to cope with him in a group. But I have the impression that these matters are decided, not by a teacher evaluating the gravity and complexity of a particular problem and saying whether she feels able personally to help that child, but by a general assumption that mentally handicapped children are automatically unacceptable in pre-school groups for normal children. I think that assumption is based on ignorance. A minority of mentally handicapped children present problems which one teacher may be able to cope with better than another, and sometimes problems which may be quite beyond the ordinary nursery school teacher. But the majority of mentally handicapped infants do not present very different needs from other pre-school children. There is no reason why services designed for pre-school children should not automatically extend to all those mentally handicapped children who could benefit from them.'

Competition with normal children. The same Journal (above) quotes information from Dr Mildred Creak on the danger of segregation, from the point of view of the realistic acceptance by parents of the child's degree of handicap. If these children are pushed into special playgroups for the handicapped the parent feels: 'We never had the chance to see how he did, in competition with normal children.'

Mixing and grouping in schools

Due to the absence from this Information Exchange Session of representatives from special schools, participants asked that a summary be included in this Report of current information on the progress being made by education authorities in grouping and mixing. This summary is provided as a footnote following the References.

Mixing and grouping in hostels, villages, hospitals and extended care homes

Hostels

London Borough of Hackney. Detailed information was given on policy and practice in the grouping and mixing of children in community provisions. A residential establishment was described with 40 places, originally intended for 20 short- stay and 20 long-stay children. In accord with the Borough's policy of 'community merging' the provision is called neither a home nor a hostel: it is simply referred to as '32–34, Brownswood Road'. The fact that it appears large reflects the Borough's problem in securing individual small sites and the necessary staff for a greater number of units. Various aspects of mixing and grouping were described. Also details were given of how assessment was made, with regard to various factors, such as chronological (birthday), physical, mental, emotional and social age; mixing and grouping for the benefit of the child was a complex matter and depended also upon the kind of staff, and the arrangement of space available.

Adults: Practices of mixing and grouping in the Borough, with reference to adults were also described and some of the recommendations made by the Department of Health and Social Security were summarised: (1) initial stages with large groups until they become familiar with setting, then, (2) formation of small groups by spontaneous grouping of residents (3) intimate living situations with some beginning to live independently and (4) degrees of autonomy as stable involvement in local community develops; these groups will not be static and will be free to adjust to the needs of the individuals.

Villages

In the absence of participants from village communities, the following references were requested.

Botton Village. The Camphill Village Trust, Botton, Danby, Nr. Whitby, Yorkshire. 'Phone Castleton (Yorkshire) 281. Principal: Peter Roth. Groupings of 8 to 16 persons in 23 houses on 430 acres. Groupings

29

are usually families with their own children and 5 to 9 mentally retarded adults. Work groupings in six workshops, four farms, gardens and households. Individuals mix voluntarily according to leisure activities and interests.

Blackerton Village. Cottage and Rural Enterprises, Blackerton House, East Anstey, Nr. Tiverton, Devon. 'Phone: Anstey Mills 252. Director: Peter Forbes. One of several projects run by CARE. Emphasis here is not on work, but on providing the retarded through suitable mixing and grouping with (*a*) personal privacy and (*b*) the development of normal relationships between staff, the villagers and their local community.

Hospitals for the Mentally Handicapped

Oxford Regional Hospital Board (now Oxford RHA). Information was provided on groupings made by kinds of disability: the congenital and respiratory who need sustained nursing care; the severely subnormal physically handicapped who are not ill, for whom work, training, social training and rehabilitative treatment is required; and the moderate or severely mentally handicapped with behaviour disorders, who will need appropriate management and work on behaviour modification. These groupings represented only a small number of the total hospital population. About 300 out of 500 patients should not be in hospital at all: they should be in local authority hostels; none of these places were yet available. On the basis of this information at least one Consultant (unnamed) had suggested that the hospitals should be handed over to the social service departments responsible.

Limits to mixing and grouping. Whilst examples were given of hospitals mixing sexes with beneficial effects and no problems others spoke of great difficulty with mixing. In general these do not try to mix by sex: they mix by disability. The point, made by several contributors from hospitals, was that any effective mixing and grouping that is possible, will depend upon the kinds of handicap and behaviour difficulty the hospital has to contain; patients on court orders, with deviant sexual behaviour, and with aggression and similar problems, were mentioned.

Family groupings. A Family Unit at Leavesden Hospital was described; babies and children; mothers and fathers; aunts and uncles and grandfathers and grandmothers. As with all the contributors of information from the hospitals, there were so many questions from interested participants for details and background to these developments, that it was not possible, in the time available, for participants to make adequate response. In the questions arising from this contribution, it was wondered if, in view of the resort to masturbation all patients segregated from community life naturally have, is it not cruel to match them, through family groupings, and then deny them sexual outlet. Masturbatory habits, if disturbed, can lead to violent behavioural problems.

This question, and many similar questions arising from the contributions made by participants from hospitals (not answered due to lack of time) made it clear that in a single Information Session it was not possible for contributors to provide sufficient information in the detail that was required. This could only be obtained by participants by direct enquiry after the Session to the individual concerned (see List of Participants).

The Brigg Report: Hospitals as 'Ghettos'? It was suggested that government policy would lead to a situation where only the 'unacceptable' would be left in hospitals. Hospitals would become 'Ghettos'. The Brigg Report held out no hope for offsetting this situation. It was thought that there was need for a conference – or a seminar – on the implications of the Brigg Report for the future of hospitals for the mentally handicapped.

Extended care homes

Information was provided on mixing and grouping in three of the NSMHC Extended Care Homes. These homes are not designed as demonstration projects, but are provided to relieve the emergency needs, arising from present gaps, due to the reorganisation of the statutory services for mentally handicapped children. One of their particular aims is to provide relief to parents suffering family stress. The three Extended Care Homes are Orchard Dene (Liverpool). Pirates' Spring (Kent), and Hales House (Norfolk). All homes cater for boys and girls, and the age limits are, respectively 13, 16 and 17 years. The NSMHC Accommodation Officer provided the following note:

'Whilst all the children who are admitted into our homes are severely subnormal their behaviour patterns and physical handicaps vary considerably. Therefore it is felt that it is in the best interests of the children, expecially the physically handicapped, that we segregate as much as possible to avoid any accidents which might otherwise occur. By doing this all the children get some attention, whereas if they were in one large group the more lively children would place such demands on the staff and would inevitably get more attention than the quieter more handicapped children. At Pirates' Spring and Orchard Dene complete segregation is in practice, whereas at Hales House the facilities do not enable segregation. Due to the limited play facilities not such a wide range of handicapped children can be accommodated. However, at Hales House – unlike the other two homes – twelve of the more lively children go out to school and the remainder have a teacher who calls daily. Out of school the children are not separated at all.'

Discussion

It was noted that the majority of the severely subnormal live at home.

Some of them are able to mix and group according to activity and capacity, much as we do. With family, friends and neighbours; through work, pastimes and hobbies. Should *all* the mentally handicapped be given a chance to do this sort of thing? What information sources were available on this? It was clear that reference to the 'mentally handicapped' as a generic group, tended to confuse the issue, and that it was necessary to define the group under consideration. In contrast to the subnormal who live at home there will be those who live in hospital: these are the group referred to as awaiting community placement. This hospital population would be likely to fall into three main sub-groupings; those who would gain open employment and seek an independent life, those for whom sheltered work would be needed and those for whom, at present, neither sheltered nor open employment could be undertaken. It was not known to what degree social competence may relate to work competence. It is possible, however, that the range of supportive services for the group (as a whole) will spread from complete independence to perhaps the need for one-to-one supportive services. It was also noted that any one of the three groups might include persons where the primary handicap (under community exposure) may turn out to be disturbed behaviour, rather than the kind or degree of mental handicap. Reference was made here to an article by a parent about her son Michael, a young adult, now in a hospital for the mentally handicapped. She states: 'Clearly if it was not so difficult I should have my son home'.

Stress at home. For 53 severely handicapped adults who were kept at home a recent survey shows that:—

24 were not left on their own for more than 5 minutes,
19 were not left on their own for more than 1 hour,
29 were unable to wash themselves,
and only 17 attended training centres.

A problem of crisis proportions. Experience has shown that returned hospital patients are unlikely to benefit from mixing and grouping with the public unless intensive community support is available. This does not at present exist. 'Unless greater priority is given to the plight of the mentally handicapped (those for whom the protection of hospitals are no longer provided) the problem may reach crisis proportions'. The responsibility of the social services were underlined. If the handicapped are to be kept out of segregated hospitals (and units) to continue life in the community, then effective domiciliary services must be provided. If, on the other hand, those already segregated from the community are to return, this same provision, plus adequate half-way hostels, and social work support, must be provided. Training must also be given in hostels. They must not be used for 'storage' places, for those who have lost their parents, and for whom there are no longer places available elsewhere. The question was also raised as to what the proportion was of those who failed to group and mix with the normal community because their capacity to adjust had been impaired by segregation (institutionalisation) as compared with those who failed simply because community supportive services did not yet exist for them. Again, with regard to this specific group, the further issue was raised: 'Is public opinion – and perhaps some professional opinion as well – a product of segregation?' It had been noted that the 'public' would petition against a hostel being built in their road. The public were often cruel, yet a neighbour, with a single handicapped member, is often treated with consideration and sympathy. There is a need for further information on this. It was suggested, however, that individuals, lacking proper social competence, being returned to community life, without effective support could mean that, even as individuals (rather than groups) they could possibly prejudice public opinion.

Mixing and grouping for living

The aim of this Session was to fill gaps in information available on mixing and grouping. Many examples were given, but little was said of the theory or aim which – long term – lay behind these methods. Was some mixing and grouping simply a response to the limits set by the present inadequate provisions? On closing the Morning Session the Session Editor said he had an uneasy feeling that some of the participants, in talking about mixing and grouping, tended to look at the handicapped as 'collections of problems'. He also quoted: 'Mentally handicapped children and adults should not be segregated unnecessarily from other people of similar age'.

A lively exchange of information, with which the Session closed, was due almost entirely to the contributions of two Authors. The Afternoon Session had opened with summaries of these. The first reported upon a survey of the physically handicapped; they wanted to stay at home. They did not wish to be segregated in the new hospital units, now being provided, often at far distant places, which would cut them off from friends, neighbours and relatives. It was noted that a survey of hostels (in Lancashire) showed that most of the mentally handicapped residents

33

would prefer to be at home. The second paper dealt with integration or segregation of the mentally handicapped and provided valuable statistical material – also listing a wide range of further references to this topic. Following a discussion of this paper there was a certain amount of misunderstanding and it was explained that the Paper was in no way critical of the way the pressing problems of the present were being dealt with, by the participants. Waiting lists for hostels and severe overcrowding; staff shortages, and similar problems; these were being valiantly met. It was wished, however, that these grievous conditions could be removed in the future. This could be done only by proper planning and spending. Expenditure upon inappropriate building programmes must be avoided. This planning needed to be done now.

Grouping for marriage. The pressing need was outlined of young married couples (mentally handicapped) for whom no training for living was available. A project was badly needed. An example of work with young married couples, not necessarily handicapped, which could be useful for further study was the Frimhurst Recuperative Home and Readjustment Centre, Frimley Green, Aldershot, Hants. (Mrs R. Goodman). Another interesting development, half completed was the London Borough of Newham's Cundy House, Garvary Road, E16. 'Phone 511 0126. Warden: Mrs S. Gill. Here separate bed-sitting rooms and small flats would provide a preparation for independent living. This development could possibly be suitable for the training of young married couples.

Mixing and grouping for leisure and therapy

Leisure Clubs:

The Administration Secretary, National Federation of Gateway Clubs, due to absence from the Session reports as follows:

'The Federation has no fixed policy on mixing or grouping, by age, sex, degree of handicap, mixing with other handicaps, or of mixing with normal children and adults. Each Club Leader is free to develop methods suited to the kind of membership, area density, staff, equipment and accommodation available.

High and low density areas. In areas of high density a number of clubs may exist which will be grouped by age – children; teenagers; adults. No clubs are grouped by sex or by degrees of handicap ESN, ESN (Severe). In areas of low population, all ages, and all handicaps (for which special provision does not exist) will bring about a mixed group differing in age, sex and kind or degree of handicap (for example ESN and ESN (Severe), the physically handicapped etc.). Also, although the

34

mixing of normal with handicapped is not a policy matter, many clubs encourage this through the use of volunteers and helpers from the community who merge with the handicapped members.

Activity grouping. Ideally grouping is spontaneous, and is based on activity groupings; that is, the individuals wish to join in certain activities, irrespective of age, sex, kind or degree of handicap. There are now over 300 Gateway Clubs in towns, villages and hospitals in England and Wales. Enquiries regarding specific methods of grouping and mixing will be referred to Club Leaders known to be practising them. Contact National Federation of Gateway Clubs (via NSMHC).'

Holidays

The Holiday Facilities Development Officer NSMHC explained that his role was to develop, organise and run, ad-hoc holidays for mentally handicapped children and adults, in rented or borrowed premises. This Scheme has replaced earlier NSMHC policy of providing holiday accommodation in their own residential homes. The first year in which the Scheme was carried through four projects were run, giving holidays to 90 children and adults. Subsequently the provisions have been substantially increased.

The following written notes were provided:—

Premises used were: (a) Two boarding special schools for special care holidays (1 for children, 1 for adults) where the guests often have severe physical handicaps and epilepsy as well as severe mental retardation. (b) A converted farmhouse in Cornwall for an 'adventure' type holiday for 20 high grade SSN children. (c) A guest house in Margate for 24 ESN-type adults.

Present feeling is that each holiday should provide for a narrow range of abilities and handicap, since in the holiday situation, using volunteer helpers, so much attention must be devoted to the special care cases that high grade mentally handicapped people would suffer a lack of attention. This must not, however, rule out the possibilities of integrating people of very mixed abilities on holidays in the future.

Within the context of each holiday, the guests or 'campers' are usually split up into groups of 5–8 with 3–4 volunteer helpers per group, who have responsibility for all child care duties within the group. Groups usually go through a timetable of activities during the day e.g. painting, walking, swimming, outdoor and indoor games, watching TV, physiotherapy. This applies less to holidays for higher grade people where volunteers are either individually responsible for 2 or 3 children, or work as a team collectively responsible for all of the 'campers'.

The bedrooms are the only areas where there is segregation based on

35

sex, otherwise there is total mixing, each group having a balance of handicap within it to share the overall load.

Eating takes place in a single room/area, some or all of the helpers eating with and helping the children.

Mixing of abilities, sexes and ages can be important within a defined ability range as this may:—

(i) Tend to promote a social responsibility and sense of attachment to others of similar abilities.

(ii) Teach a sense of competition to help improve abilities and techniques, and at the same time:—

(iii) Make for a helpful disposition towards less able colleagues.

(iv) Be an aid to volunteers (and make for variety) where some of their charges are less demanding in their basic needs; e.g. incontinence, feeding, etc.

There may in future be a case for running holidays covering a large spectrum of abilities even to the extent of mixing handicapped children with 'normal' children. Points to be noted here:—

(a) This may broaden the outlook and experience and knowledge of both the normal and the handicapped children.

(b) It may broaden the scope of activities possible on the holidays.

(c) It would increase public knowledge of the holidays or of the cause of the mentally handicapped in general.

(d) It may lighten the load of the volunteers.

There are however possible disadvantages:—

(a) The reduction of the number of possible holiday placements for mentally handicapped people if these places are taken up by normal holiday guests.

(b) It may diminish the attention received by the handicapped children from the helpers.

(c) It may promote a sense of incompetence in some of the mentally handicapped when they compare themselves with normal people of the same age.

(d) A possibly patronising attitude will be taken by the normal holiday-makers.

Nevertheless, this mixing may be something worth trying, but not until many more holiday places are available, and more experience is gained with degrees of mixing.

Therapeutic Leisure

Drama. A representative of Sesame gave information on the work of her organisation; they group in a variety of ways depending upon kind and degree of handicap to achieve the best therapeutic response. Seven voluntary workers offer demonstrations at evenings and week-ends providing travelling expenses can be met. Not too great an audience is preferred and work has been done with spastics, geriatrics, multiple handicaps etc.

The therapies: a need for further information sources. There is a lack of information, not only in respect of the best forms of mixing and grouping for therapeutic leisure, but also on the proper application of these to those who need them. There is also a lack of information on good practice in co-ordination; for example, for riding, swimming, gymnastics, sport, art, handicrafts (occupational) and also in the use of adventure playgrounds.

The Session Editor writes:

It was clear from the deliberations of the meeting that no ideal mix can be recommended empirically and I doubt whether such a thing would be refined by research. It is my personal hope that no such precisely defined condition exists.

If we can choose our friends and activities according to our personal likes and dislikes I hope that, in time, we shall be able to give full recognition to the dignity and status of the mentally handicapped and afford them the same privilege.

Thank you for your interest and support and making it, for me, a most enjoyable and informative day.

David Purrett.

Individual contributions are identified by page and line number on the List of Participants. References are identified by page and line, in the same way.

Participants Lists give the name, address, telephone number and post held at the time the contribution was made.

LIST OF PARTICIPANTS

SESSION EDITOR:

PURRETT, D. A.   Assistant Director of Social Services
(Residential and Day Care), City of Oxford Social Services
Department, 77–79 George Street, Oxford OX1 2BH
Telephone: Oxford 49811   Ext: 305

PARTICIPANTS

CLARK, MISS K.   Accommodation Officer, Residential Services   31–32   17– 2
Department, NSMHC, Pembridge Hall, 17 Pembridge Square,
London W2 4EP
Telephone 01-229 8941   Ext: 30

CUNNINGTON, MRS. M. H.   Nursing Officer, Bromham Hospital,   30   25–26
Near Bedford, Bedfordshire
Telephone: 023-02 2095   Ext: 35

FLETCHER, SISTER FIONA   Assistant-in-Charge, The National   27–28   17– 4
Children's Home, Ebley House, 235 Westwood Road, Ebley,
Nr. Stroud, Gloucestershire GL5 45Y
Telephone: 04-536 4307

FOSTER, B.   Charge Nurse, Farleigh Hospital, Flax Bourton, Bristol,   30   27–32
BS19 3QZ   31   11–16
Telephone: Flax Bourton 2028   33   14–16

GARLICK, MRS. E.   Assistant Supervisor of Brian Didsbury
Training Centre, London Borough of Newham, 99 The Grove,   34   9–24
Stratford, London E15 1HR
Telephone: 01-534 4545   Ext: 238

HABIEB, P.   Superintendent, Handicapped Unit, London Borough   29   6–19
of Hackney, 32/34 Brownswood Road, London N4   30–31   40– 4
Telephone: 01-800 2256

HAWES, MISS K.   Instructor, Chelmsford Adult Training Centre
c/o Miss R. M. Lang, Principal Officer, Social Services
Department, County Council of Essex, Kensal House, 77
Springfield Road, Chelmsford CM2 6JG
Telephone: 02-45 67181   Ext: 261

HAWORTH, W.   Mental Health Advisor Social Services, Westminster
City Hall, Victoria Street, London SW1
Telephone 01-828 8070   Ext: 2432

HEPPER, MRS. A.   Social Worker, Advisory Casework Services,   28   5– 6
National Association for Mental Health, 39 Queen Anne Street,   34   13–19
London W1M 0AV
Telephone: 01-935 1272

HUNT, MISS H.   Assistant Regional Officer, NSMHC, Metropolitan
Region, Coventry House, 5–6 Coventy Street, London W1
Telephone: 01-437 4538

HURGON, MRS. I. Organising Secretary, 'Sesame', George Bell   36–37   38– 4
House, 8 Ayres Street, London SE1
Telephone: 01-407 2158

REFERENCES

	page	lines

GRAY FRANKLIN, G. 'Holding down a job: helping the mentally handicapped succeed in open employment' (September 1973) 'Parent's Voice': The Journal of the NSMHC. — page 25, lines 20

MORRIS, P. 'Put away: a sociological study of institutions for the mentally retarded' (1969) Routledge and Kegan Paul. — page 26, lines 4

DYBWAD, G. 'The mentally handicapped child under five' (Reprint 1973) NSMHC. — page 28, lines 4

PRE-SCHOOL PLAYGROUPS ASSOCIATION: 'Handicapped children in playgroups' (1972). — page 28, lines 8

FAULKNER, R. E. 'Opportunity classes and community care' (March 31st 1973) Health and Social Services Journal. — page 28, lines 8

BRYANT, P., MITTLER, P. and O'CONNOR, N. 'The handicapped child: recent research findings' (1971) The College of Special Education. — page 29, lines 4

DEPARTMENT OF EDUCATION AND SCIENCE: 'Diagnostic and assessment units: Education Survey 9' (1970) HMSO. — page 29, lines 4

DEPARTMENT OF EDUCATION AND SCIENCE: 'Slow learners in secondary schools: Education Survey 15' (1968) HMSO. — page 29, lines 4

DEPARTMENT OF EDUCATION AND SCIENCE: 'Aspects of special education, schools for delicate children, special classes in ordinary schools: Education Survey 17' (1972) HMSO. — page 29, lines 4

DEPARTMENT OF EDUCATION AND SCIENCE: 'Report on education: No. 77' (1973) Department of Education and Science. — page 29, lines 4

THE FOUNTAIN VALLEY SCHOOL: 'Children without labels: handicapped children in the regular classroom' (1972) The Fountain Valley School District Project, Fountain Valley, California 92708, U.S.A. — page 29, lines 4

DEPARTMENT OF EDUCATION AND SCIENCE AND DEPARTMENT OF HEALTH AND SOCIAL SECURITY: 'Joint draft circular SS/13/30/02': (1973) DES and DHSS. — page 29, lines 4

UNITED KINGDOM MENTAL HEALTH FILM COUNCIL: 'Whose handicapped' (1972) A film from Concord Film Council. — page 29, lines 4

PILKINGTON, T. A. 'Guide to films on mental handicap' (1973) NSMHC. — page 29, lines 4

GEORGE PEABODY TEACHERS' COLLEGE: 'A time to learn' Nashville, Tennessee, U.S.A. (From Hester Adrian Research Centre, University of Manchester). — page 29, lines 4

DEPARTMENT OF HEALTH AND SOCIAL SECURITY: 'Residential accommodation for mentally handicapped adults: local authority building note 8' (1973) Welsh Office, HMSO. — page 29, lines 28

DEPARTMENT OF HEALTH AND SOCIAL SECURITY: 'Report on a committee on nursing' (1972) Chairman: Professor Asa Briggs. Cmnd 5115 HMSO. — page 31, lines 14

DEPARTMENT OF HEALTH AND SOCIAL SECURITY: 'Better services for the mentally handicapped' (1971) Cmnd Paper 4683 HMSO. — page 31, lines 13

GRAY, E. 'A parent's voice' (September 1973) APEX *The Journal of the Institute of Mental Subnormality*. — page 32, lines 26

BAYLEY, M. 'Mental handicap and community care' (1973) Routledge and Kegan Paul. — page 32, lines 32

MARAIS, E. 'Cast adrift' (9th August 1973) New Society. — page 32, lines 38

MIXING AND GROUPING IN SCHOOLS

Participants requested that a brief guide should be provided to the references showing their relevance to the mixing and grouping of handicapped children in ordinary schools: these notes are given below:

RESEARCH

'*The handicapped child: recent research findings' Peter Bryant, Peter Mittler, and Neil O'Connor.*

Dr Beate Hermelin, in introducing these papers says: 'If you think you know the answers . . . to motivational, attentional and intellectual learning deficits in children, when in fact you do not, you are likely to make mistakes. . . . You may even fail to recognise the answers when they do emerge'. These papers are all written in a language easily understood by any discipline. With regard to mixing and grouping of children Dr O'Connor's paper 'General and Specific Deficits', may be thought to have particular relevance.

SURVEYS

'*Diagnostic and assessment units: education survey 9'.*

Grouping and kinds of handicaps. It is suggested that '. . . the presence of the children in these units inevitably limits the opportunities open to them to experience the ordinary everyday things of life on which so much of their subsequent learning will depend'.

'*Slow learners in secondary schools: education survey 15'.*

This Survey (1967–68) covers an investigation into the success of ordinary schools in providing for children with an apparent variety of handicapping conditions.

'*Aspects of special education. Schools for delicate children. Special classes in ordinary schools: education survey 17'.*

Shows how 'an established system of special education has gradually adapted itself to new demands and changing beliefs'. Describes how special classes can provide 'the care and attention a handicapped child needs without withdrawing him from his normal school'.

REPORTS

Report on education: Number 77'.

This Report restates Departmental Policy that no handicapped child should attend a special school—if his needs can be met by an ordinary school; that the grouping and mixing of children (placement) should depend upon individual need and not on category of disability. Useful statistics are provided. For example, of children suffering 'mental or educational backwardness' (Isle of Wight Survey), 134 per 1,000 (13.4%) were receiving or would benefit from special help in an ordinary school.

REPORTS FROM OVERSEAS

'*Children without labels: handicapped children in the regular classroom.*

This 66 page Report describes Project Number 0135 (907 pupils). Report states (page 19) 'at the conclusion of the Project all handicapped students were successfully integrated into regular classroom programmes'. Report includes details of kinds of handicap, a full evaluation of results, and a selected bibliography.

GUIDANCE
'*The education of mentally handicapped children and young people in hospital*'.
A Draft proposed and widely circulated for comment. Will replace the guidance given in Circular 312 (1956). Provides information on mixing and grouping, with particular reference to the roles of nurses and teachers.

FILMS
United Kingdom Mental Health Film Council: 'Whose handicapped?' (1972) Colour. 34 mins. From Concord Film Council. Shows normal and mentally handicapped children mixing together. This, and similar films, are listed in: 'Guide to films on mental handicap' Thomas A. Pilkington (1973) NSMHC Bookshop. A film, not yet listed, but specially recommended by Mr Peter Moss, was 'A time to learn' colour. 28 mins. from Dr J. Hogg, Hester Adrian Research Centre, University of Manchester. M13 9PL. Phone 061-273 3333.

Deals with 'The Toddler Research and Interaction Project', for pre-school normal and mentally handicapped children (mixed) at the George Peabody Teachers' College, Nashville, Tennessee, U.S.A.

THE EVALUATION OF HOSTELS

Session Editor: Dr Alison Rosen, MA PhD

Dr Rosen, with the support of the Department of Health and Social Security, has been responsible for a series of research projects, which has included studies on hostels for mentally handicapped adults.

Provisions for children

Department of Health and Social Security (Provisions under local directors of social service)

Cambridgeshire (Northern Area). This authority was trying to develop 3 projects simultaneously, one of which was a hostel for the under-sixteens. It was particularly important that the pressure on parents of young children should be relieved. There should be provision for day relief and week-end relief for parents of the pre-school child so that parents could enjoy a social life and know the child was being properly cared for.

Education and Social Services

The Assistant Education Officer (Primary and Special Schools), London Borough of Redbridge Education Department, said that the only residential provision for severely subnormal children was provided by Dr Barnardo: most of these children attend local special schools. The remainder of the severely subnormal children in the Borough are accommodated in hospitals outside the Borough and most of these attend hospital schools. The Social Services Department have plans for providing a hostel for 15–20 children. Should hostels for the severely subnormal be the responsibility of social services, or education?

Part-time changes to full-time care. A Senior Social Worker (East Sussex) said that two small children's hostels, one purpose-built, and one a converted house, attached to a school for the ESN (Severe), had recently been ceded to West Sussex as part of county re-organisation. She said that these hostels could have been filled twice over: about one-third of the residents were children who could not easily travel the distance from

43

home to school. But it had been found that five-day care tended to stretch to seven-day care. She also mentioned training hostels, for young adults, providing residential care on a five-day or full-time basis, from which residents could go either to a training centre, or out to work. It was also noted that some parents would like 2-day care (at weekends) rather than 5-day (Monday to Friday) care. Many mothers can cope with a mentally handicapped child Monday to Friday, since the child is out of the house for a considerable part of the day, whereas Saturday and Sunday pose problems.

Lack of effective contact with school. The Senior Supervisor (Residential Care), London Borough of Wandsworth Social Services said that, with regard to a hostel for severely subnormal children, although it was on the same site, there was no effective contact with the school. He said that the 20 places in the hostel had been cut to 16, and that there were now 11 staff in the hostel for these 16 children, but there was need for an aim, apart from simply providing care. They could easily fill the hostel with long-stay children, but they wished to reserve places for parents whose children required local education. When parents agree to short-stay for their children, this often turns to long-stay. By providing short-stay, staff think they are strengthening the bonds of the family; in fact, they are weakening them. This point was clarified after the Session. He thought it was possible that parents who resist the provision of short-stay care are the ones who wish to keep their children at home, whilst some of the parents, but not all, who accept short-term care, are those who wish to have their children permanently cared for away from home, but hesitate to do this, until short-term care is offered them. One of the problems was staffing difficulties. The Borough had long-term plans for a specialised adolescent unit, and also a long-stay hostel for 10–15 adults or, as an alternative, small warden-controlled flats for 5 to 6 people.

Department of Health and Social Security: National Health Service: (Provisions under regional hospital boards)

A hostel under a hospital board. A Nursing Officer, Castle Hill House (Dorset) explained that this was a residential hostel for 25 severely subnormal children, now under the Regional Hospital Board but, under NHS reorganisation, is to be attached to a general hospital. Only 19 children are accommodated at present, and there are three beds for short-stay children and one bed for emergency care. The children are mainly long-stay and a programme of education and rehabilitation concentrates on developing the five senses: there are both individual and group behaviour modification programmes. There is a total staff of 22, made up of two teachers, two physiotherapists, and 18 house parents. The hostel also provides day-care, parent and child guidance, and there is an attached social worker for each child. A major fault was that there was no career structure for the child-care staff. The school-leaving age of the severely subnormal should not be based upon birthday age, but should be based instead on mental age.

The work of Dr Albert Kushlick. The Session Editor pointed out that the Castle Hill House Hostel (described above) was set up according to a blueprint developed by Dr Kuschlick under the Wessex Regional Hospital Board (now Wessex RHA). According to the Kushlick blueprint the children at Castle Hill House would not be selected in terms of their capacity to benefit from any particular regimen but would simply be any and all children from the specified catchment area for Castle Hill House whose parents were not able or willing to have them at home.

Department of Education and Science: (Provisions under local education authorities)

School-linked hostels needed. A Head Teacher, (Orchard Court Special School: Cambridgeshire) emphasised the need for hostels for the severely subnormal category of child. He thought such provision was important when dealing with parents as they should be able to go out at night. He said that at times of illness of the mother, children at present have to go into care in the large hospitals: help should always be available to these parents in the community. Parents should also be given the opportunity to leave their children in residential care during holidays, so that they can take a holiday without them if they so wish.

A narrow dividing line between educational care and residential care. A Head Teacher, (The Rees Thomas School, also in Cambridgeshire, but in the south of the County), said that he had 12 children in a small hostel, but it was only open when the school was open. The children are admitted mainly to relieve difficult home situations: a minority are admitted for educational reasons. This hostel is under the local Education Authority, not the Social Services Department, since the school 'day' of 6 hours is not sufficient to help them with social adaptation. Some of the children are provided with places in normal children's residential homes and the Social Services Department are planning to build a small children's hostel in 1976. Noting the contribution made by earlier participants (i.e. the need for parent relief) he thought there was a very narrow dividing line between the children's need for residential care with a bias toward the education of the child, and full-time care as would be provided by a hostel under the Social Services Department.

45

ILEA. a model of its kind. The Head Teacher, Great Stoney School (Essex) described what appeared to be a model of its kind. A boarding special school (under the Inner London Education Authority but sited in Essex) providing residential schooling for 185 ESN and 20 ESN (Severe) boys and girls age 7 to 16 years. There are eight boarding cottages and there are 128 staff. Attempts had been made (residentially) to integrate the ESN with the ESN (S) but this was not satisfactory. One reason for this was that the ESN often made progress and went on to normal schools, whilst the ESN (S) remained until school-leaving: this gave a large differential in age to the groups. The children live in the cottages with child-care staff who are non-teachers (5 staff to 20 children). There is co-operation in social education, and in evening leisure activities, between teachers and care staff. With these provisions no special problems in keeping staff had been experienced.

The teachers' feelings about status could be a problem: just as many teachers feel that there is a higher status teaching in a grammar school (rather than in a comprehensive) so certain teachers also feel that teaching the ESN is a higher status job than teaching the ESN (S). There was a need for some sort of holiday accommodation (a special hostel?) for children from his school who have no homes to go to during the holidays (when his residential school closes down). At present such children are in the unfortunate position of having to return to subnormality hospitals. A further point should be raised: should hostels for the ESN (S) carry through to adult age so that late development could still be fostered by an educational approach.

The non-statutory services

The National Society for Mentally Handicapped Children. The Matron, Pirate's Spring, NSMHC Residential Centre, said that she provided extended residential care for 24 severely subnormal children, age 0 to 16 years; these children are sent to her from 17 different local authorities: she thought this was a reflection of the fact that these authorities either did not have suitable residential provisions themselves, or that staff in such premises were not prepared to accept the very 'low grade' child. Two qualified teachers were provided for the Pirate's Spring Residential Centre by the Kent Education Authority.

These grievously disabled children needed the right kind of love, or they would not get the stimulation they needed. It had been the intention of the NSMHC to close Pirate's Spring but pressure from parents was such that it had been decided to keep the home open for an indefinite period. Had Pirate's Spring been closed it was clear these extended care children would not have returned to their homes: they would have had to be admitted into hospitals as there was nowhere else for them to go. It was this kind of child who would need, at the age of 16, some kind of permanent home, as an alternative to hospital care, throughout their adult lives.

Provisions for Adults

Department of Health and Social Security: (Provisions under local directors of social service)

Blocking of adult training hostels highlights lack of comprehensive services. A manager (Roehampton Hostel) said that he was responsible for a 30 bed hostel that serves a Borough population of 300,000. A decision had been made to admit high-grade mentally handicapped adults in order to achieve a quick through-put. He said that now that the residents were ready to leave there was nowhere for them to go. He felt that they had been 'slipping up' in providing effective counselling for families and this was now being stepped-up. He thought we tended to present our mentally handicapped as 'curiosities'. We continually over-emphasise care and support. We accept 'sentimental' attitudes. Why is it that we do not present (the majority ?) of the mentally handicapped as people – and as 'contributors' to our society. He felt that most of us had a strange way of presenting our case to the community. In particular, he thought that the fact that training hostels tend to become 'storage places' is due to the fact that we are not offering the mentally handicapped a comprehensive service.

For one kind of comprehensive service in a London Borough see 'Employment'. (Page 107).

Link between school and hostel. The Head Teacher, the John F. Kennedy School (Inner London Education Authority) said that a hostel for the under 16's was about to be built in her Borough (Newham). For the pupils staying on over the age of sixteen in her school, who are already accommodated in the Borough's Adult Hostel, an on-going programme of social education is projected by the teachers out to the hostel (i.e. practical work with money and menus; also adult education). She also referred to the residential services being provided in her own Borough for mentally handicapped adults, in several stages, or levels.

A hostel in a private house. A Principal Social Worker, London Borough of Sutton described provision made for 12 men (a large house in two flats) age range 18–58, for both subnormal and severely subnormal, with some having multiple handicaps (epilepsy, schizophrenia, etc.). The Hostel is under the supervision of a Charge Nurse from Manor Hospital, Epsom. The Hostel was in the middle of the 'stockbroker belt' and careful attention was given to good public relations. The hostel could be described as multi-purpose in that lots of neighbourhood social functions and meetings are held on the premises; neighbours can leave their children in the care of hostel staff for a few hours if need be; staff will help sick neighbours etc. There is a strong emphasis on integration with the local community. The Borough has plans for future building, and when a second hostel opens both it and the hostel already described will become mixed-sex establishments.

An adult community 'hostel'. The Officer in Charge, Prospect House Hostel, Southampton, said his local authority were due to open this hostel, (25 places for mixed adults). He was aware of applicants with all degrees of handicap, age 18 to 60 years; he felt this residential provision is only scratching the surface of the problem. In general, the aim of Prospect House would be to see the hostel as a continuation of training. There would be a flat in the hostel, for use in group work and as a bridge to life in group houses in the community.

Group homes in the community. The first speaker in the Morning Session, a Senior Social Worker (Northern Area) Cambridgeshire, had mentioned a purpose-built hostel for 25 adults and a group home for adults being set up in conjunction with a local voluntary organisation in a re-decorated ex-police house. An Area Officer, also Northern Area Cambridgeshire, said that some members of voluntary societies, (mainly parents of the mentally handicapped) resist change which might benefit their members. The group home was a case in point. Some parents are reluctant to accept that mentally handicapped adults might be able to live without constant supervision (the proposed group home would have no staff on the premises but considerable social work support and supervision).

A hospital training hostel in the community. A Charge Nurse, Leavesden Hospital and his wife, a Nursing Assistant, Leavesden Hospital, provided further information on the community hostel belonging to the Hospital Board (in Watford), for which they are responsible. The aim of this hostel is to train for community life, and thus provide a bridge from institutional discipline to self-discipline. This is a project closely linked to the rehabilitation services provided within Leavesden Hospital. The original aim of this hostel was that patients should be given six months residential training for independence. If successful, they would go out into the community: if unsuccessful they would return to the hospital for further rehabilitation treatment. In fact, due to lack of co-operation from local authorities, there are not sufficient placements being made in the community for those ready to leave, and so the hostel is becoming 'blocked' and is not achieving its intended aim.

A different aim. A Nursing Assistant, Leavesden Hospital and his wife, Housekeeper, Nascot Grange were together responsible for running a hostel (also under Leavesden Hospital) for 12 male residents. In contrast to the hostel in Watford, described above (for women only), the aim of this hostel is to provide for the men, who are mainly in open employment, a supportive residential home life.

The Royal Earlswood Hospital. A Ward Sister, Royal Earlswood Hospital described the progress being made in the rehabilitation of patients with a view to their further placement according to progress.

A proposed accreditation scheme

A paper, outlining a proposed accreditation scheme, from which the following quotation is taken, was circulated to participants:—

> 'If criteria of good residential care practice and its integration with local social and educational facilities and services could be designed, then an accreditation scheme for all residential and other services for the mentally handicapped might be developed. Such a scheme, by creating standards of optimal care, would indicate weaknesses in a particular unit compared with others, and if sufficiently sophisticated, provide a scale against which differing practices, services and accommodation might be compared.'

Evaluation and accreditation

The Session Editor opened the Afternoon Session by suggesting that you cannot begin to evaluate residential services for the mentally handicapped unless you have an aim. What was the aim of the residential provisions so far described by participants in the present Session? For children? For adults? Summarising some of the earlier contributions the Session Editor asked: 'Is it your aim to cater for all the mentally handicapped people in your area who need accommodation? If so, then what are your subsidiary aims? Simply making your residents happy, or to provide a training ground; to integrate; to normalise? If we talk about evaluation we must have clearly stated aims and ways of determining to what extent these aims are being achieved.' Different people have different aims. Will the aim of the Warden differ from that of his Director of Residential Services? What is the aim of the Department of Health and Social Security? What is the aim of the social worker? At one end of the scale of aims there will be intensive rehabilitation and education; at the other end the provision of permanence of caring and security. It is important that everyone connected with any one particular hostel agrees as to the aims of that hostel. Also, do the mentally handicapped themselves get left out? What do 'they' think, see and feel about living? For example, a self-care unit at St Ebba's Hospital is described where patients take full responsibility for themselves. These patients, whilst they would be competent for life in the community, do not wish to leave the hospital. Also, at the same hospital, patients who have been 'discharged' to the community, choose to return regularly to enjoy their holidays in the hospital setting.

Dr Alison Rosen. It was noted by participants that the Session Editor had herself undertaken a research project on hostels: the following quotation briefly reviewed this work:—

'Dr Alison Rosen, who was supported by the DHSS in a series of studies on hostels for the adult mentally handicapped provided by Lancashire County Council, outlined some of the main findings. She drew attention to the fact that some of the hostels were increasingly being used to prevent admission to hospital, at the expense of those being discharged from hospital. She also pointed out that frequently wardens of the hostels were not involved in selection procedures although they had the day-to-day responsibility for clients on admission. The clients themselves were interviewed too, and virtually all preferred hostel to hospital care, although most, however unrealistically, said they would prefer to be at home. A tendency was noted on the part of some hostel staff to encourage dependency in clients, and in Dr Rosen's view there is a need to nurture independence, possibly by the provision of group homes for those with mental handicap who can manage in this setting.'

Discussion

Hostel: (under Leavesden Hospital). The staff participating from this hostel felt their aim was very clear; to provide their girls with residential training that would take them 'from institutional discipline, to self-discipline'. The subsidiary aim was to achieve this in six months for each patient. They gave a detailed breakdown of their training programme, but explained that a further subsidiary aim was a caring and family-like atmosphere. For example, the groupings of new and old admissions was very important, and also particular attention to individual needs. A girl about to get married, was encouraged to buy the food and cook for her fiancé, who was invited to dinner on Friday nights (other examples were given). The only problem was that the hostel was now 'blocked' by girls ready to go out to local authorities who had not yet made provisions to receive them. A Monday night case conference was described where, in co-operation with the visiting psychologist, social workers and others each case is given continual assessment, with a view to deciding when the aim of the staff had been achieved, and residents were ready to 'move on'. They were surprised that there were residential projects running without well defined aims. Were these outside of the NHS? Aims could only be fully achieved with properly trained staff: aims were part of staff training. Both participants had taken teaching diplomas, for work with the adult mentally handicapped (NAMH).

The question was asked whether lack of local provisions (referred to above) might not be more quickly overcome by the provision of small community homes. The Session Editor said that there was at present little written up about these in the literature. It was noted, however, that in the Information Exchange, Return to Community Life (Page 85) there was a useful description of a Management Study based on a community home (called a Minimal Support Project) under a hospital board. There were also references to a Minimal Support Project provided by a local authority.

It was suggested that Boarding-out Schemes were a further possibility; but people were keen to have men, not women. Families did not like women; the clutter of powder, smalls and cosmetics in the bathroom; girls making cups of tea in the kitchen; women were regarded as 'rival' home-makers. The mentally handicapped could be very lonely in lodgings. Such schemes in Denbighshire had failed: integration of the handicapped with the community can only occur through gradual processes; it cannot be forced. However; it was noted from other Information Exchanges that the success or failure of supportive lodging schemes (like the success or failure of any kind of provision) was shown to depend on a variety of factors; not least of these is effective assessment.

The predicament of a typical local authority (The London Borough of Wandsworth) was described, with 110 homeless families, lack of staff, lack of building materials, and increases in the rate of rising prices. Even with an increased budget, compared with earlier years, only half the provision could be built. As a result of this situation a participant, (East Sussex), pointed out, teenagers can graduate from training, only to be put into hospital, because there is nowhere else for them to go. Had sufficient thought been given to the need for permanent residential homes for adults who were grievously handicapped and unable to undertake sheltered work, or open employment. Although permanent care may be desirable, to maintain a service where people are dependent on you is very expensive. Mention was made of existing premises that it was necessary to close down (London Borough of Sutton), because of rocketing costs. (£30,000 expenditure had been estimated to look after changes necessary to cover fire risks). In this connection participants noted the advantage of provision of permanent care in village communi-

51

ties, and the advantages of encouraging permanent staff, with a non-hierarchical structure.

The plight of parents. The plight of parents was a crucial area we were only, if at all, just beginning to understand.

The return of a resident from a Watford hostel to a situation near her family's home in Slough was described. The parents were up in arms about it. But what had been done, by way of parent counselling, to ensure that the girl would be well received by her parents, prior to the girl being placed within reach of her family home? What had been the family reasons for her original placement? A Parent who herself has a mentally handicapped daughter, described her feelings when her daughter, who had been resident at the NSMHC Slough Project for two years, was due to return again to the family home. This contribution made it very clear that the Session had not really considered the position of parents of mentally handicapped children, and of mentally handicapped adults.

Surely it was not natural for grown up sons and daughters to come back and live at home. Grown up children normally go away from home, and make their own kind of lives. Why then should those who run hostels, and work in the social services, expect parents to wish to have their grown up children back home again? This was not natural; it was not normal. It seemed that it would take a new generation to give to the mentally handicapped – and their parents – the freedom, and the respect, that both deserve.

In emphasising the stress suffered by parents a participant suggested that it was the duty of social workers, in individual cases, and where it was appropriate, to prevent the return of mentally handicapped adults back to their home areas. Having seen the stress effects on families who had managed well for many years, she knew that this stress could be more than parents were sometimes able to manage; it was also, as the previous participant, a parent, had pointed out, unnecessary. It was suggested that, mainly due to the stress that had been imposed upon the present generation of the adult mentally handicapped, they were an unnatural population. These people, when young, had either been over-protected by their families, rejected by their families, or simply 'kept' by families, because of feelings of parental guilt, which had made possible the continued tolerance of the handicapped person in the household.

A Head Teacher (Great Stoney School) said that things were still much the same. Parents' expectations are still often unrealistic; many parents still seek 'magical' cures; parents who do not feel their child is making 'progress' ask for the child to be returned home from residential schooling. There is a Parent–School Association and much effort is made to provide parent counselling, but there are some pretty difficult parents.

To 'abandon' a child to permanent residential care is a tough decision to make; parents feel their child will benefit from the love and affection that only they can give: and yet to give this to the child, means having the child at home: Cases were quoted where the return of the child to his home had to be refused; in one of these cases it was because of the presence of an unaccepting mother-in-law. This problem could only be tackled by dealing with the family situation immediately following the birth of a severely handicapped child. This meant earlier detection of severe handicap, and proper counselling services.

A participant wondered whether there could not be extended care residential establishments that also provide social centres for multiple usage (special care, day care etc.). Could these be designed to take in the needs of the whole family constellation? The Session Editor suggested that such possible multiple usage could provide, under a single roof, residential care for adults who would be out at work (or training centre) during the day and which would then permit the building to be used for the day special-care of adults living at home. The participant from Castle Hill House said that his hostel provided both day care and night residence to separate groups of children.

Home is best. If the aim of a hostel is to provide a home, it is necessary to check on our own needs. What do we ourselves consider 'homely' – ? (Nobody asks the residents!) The Roehampton Hostel is fully stretched in providing leisure in the evenings, the preparation of meals for when the residents return, etc. What would our own reaction be if we were asked to use our own homes for some other purpose during the daytime?

The Session Editor said that, in her own view, she thought it would be difficult to talk of any 25 bedded hostel as 'home'.

Hostels—who is responsible?

Health, Education, Social Services? The discussion concluded with a number of contributions which indicated that the aim of hostels, and therefore the evaluation of this aim (or aims) might be more easily discussed if either the health services, the social services, or the education authority, were seen to be central to their organisation/administration. With small family, or domestic units (see the work of Dr Kushlick, Page 45) the whole problem came right back to the quality, and stability of staff. The participant from Castle Hill House said that they had got their own Parents Association, plenty of Sunshine Coaches, a wonderful swimming pool, 13 of their 19 children need physiotherapy (and get it), and yet there is a continual shortage and turnover of staff! (6 to 12 monthly turnover). The 'life' of houseparents, as shown by the Spastics Society experience, was a very short one indeed. The Head Teacher (Great

Stoney School) said that a lot depended upon the organisation of staff and the satisfaction they are given in their job: he had no staff problems (3 years without staff turn-over). He thought the reasons for high staff turn-over in certain projects could be made the subject for useful study. The participant from the London Borough of Sutton said that staffing hostels for the mentally handicapped presented special problems. A Warden will say that a charge nurse is not properly qualified, and a charge nurse will say that a social worker is no good! It was pointed out by a Charge Nurse that, however fully qualified you may be, if you have gained your experience under Hospital Boards you must never mention this, if you want a job in community hostels!

In conclusion an effort was made to list, with the help of participants, the variety and range of residential provisions required to meet each of the aims of the present services for the mentally handicapped. Time was not available to do this in the course of the present Session.

Contribution from the Department of Health and Social Security

Observers from the Department of Health and Social Security had attended the Information Session and had carefully listened to the contributions made by participants. With the change of Government and the appointment of the new Minister, anything said by them could be subject to policy changes, but certain crucial areas could be identified for discussion. There was, for example, an increasing need for a more meaningful definition of roles, between local education authorities and social service departments, between social services and hospitals, and between nursing and care staff (The Brigg Report). Following the publication of 'Better Services for the Mentally Handicapped' (1971) the Department had been very disappointed in the lack of co-operation of local authorities with the hospital services. Priority of provisions should be 'common-ground', between hospitals and local authorities.

It was not known what line the new Minister would take, but she would have for her consideration the idea of a 'Unified Mental Handicap Service', as a way of overcoming the present gaps in the services.

Since the 1970 Education Act, certain registered children's homes were recognised as educational establishments; that is, the home remains a home, whilst at the same time being adapted as a school. An enquiry had been held recently, which was shortly to be published, and it is likely to be shown that there is need for much more scope for social service involvement.

Sir Keith Joseph had been much in favour of involving voluntary organisations and had given much encouragement in this field. A variety of grant; had been made in support of developing voluntary services connected with the mentally handicapped. It was not thought that the new Minister was likely to reverse this trend.

The Session Editor writes:

The title of this Information Exchange was 'The Evaluation of Hostels: aims, developments and schemes for accreditation'. We heard a lot about developments – recent, not-so-recent and proposed. We heard something about aims. We heard very little about schemes for accreditation, i.e. attempts to measure the quality of hostel care. It would seem that formal or systematic evaluation of hostels is as yet not often undertaken. This takes us back to aims, since it is impossible to evaluate a service unless one knows exactly what it seeks to achieve. Taking the day's discussion as a whole a number of recurrent themes emerge, e.g. staffing problems; community attitudes; possible use of hostels for short-term relief for parents (a few hours, evenings, etc.), and the 'blocking' of hostel places due to a lack of resident turnover.

What is clear is that we need a wide range of residential provision – both hostels and other forms of accommodation – for both adults and children. Only thus can we hope best to serve the needs of each and every mentally handicapped person coming into residential care.

Alison Rosen

Individual contributions are identified by page and line number on the List of Participants. References are identified by page and line, in the same way.

Participants Lists give the name, address, telephone number and post held at the time the contribution was made.

LIST OF PARTICIPANTS

SESSION EDITOR:

ROSEN, DR ALISON, MA PhD   Research Psychologist,
56 Warren Road, Wanstead, London E11
Telephone: 01-989 5224

PARTICIPANTS

BARNES, R.   Head Teacher, Great Stoney School, Chipping
Ongar, Essex
Telephone: Ongar 2027

BROUGH, MRS. M.   Matron, Pirate's Spring, NSMHC Residential
Centre, St Mary's Bay, New Romney, Kent
Telephone: 06793 3351

CAIN, MISS MARGARET   Secretarial Assistant, British Association
for the Retarded, 17 Pembridge Square, London W2 4EP
Telephone: 01-229 8941

CONE, F.   Nursing Officer, Castle Hill House, Parkstone, Poole,
Dorset
Telephone: Parkstone 747416

DOBSON, MISS C. J.   Area Officer of Social Services Department,
Northern Area Cambridgeshire and Isle of Ely Social Services,
County Hall, March, Cambridgeshire
Telephone: March 2471   Ext: 28

FAIRBROTHER, MRS. P.   Vice-Chairman, NSMHC, 170 Queens
Road, London SW19
Telephone: 01-540 5919

GELLATLY, MRS. V.   Ward Sister, Royal Earlswood Hospital,
Redhill, Surrey RH1 6JL
Telephone: Redhill 63591

HAYMAN, MRS. OLIVE   Principal Social Worker, Social Services
Department, London Borough of Sutton, Town Hall,
Wallington, Surrey
Telephone: 01-669 0011

KAVANAGH, P.   Manager, Roehampton Hostel, 230 Roehampton
Lane, London SW15
Telephone: 01-789 0740

LEACH, MISS M. B.   Assistant Regional Officer, NSMHC South
West Region, 17 High Street, Taunton, Somerset
Telephone: 0823 2836

LINDLEY, D. N.   Assistant Education Officer, (Primary and Special
Schools), London Borough of Redbridge Education Department,
Lynton House, 255–259 High Road, Ilford, Essex
Telephone: 01-478 3020   Ext: 387

MADDEN, P.   Senior Supervisor (Residential Care), London
Borough of Wandsworth Social Services Department, 61 High
Street, London SW18
Telephone: 01-870 0071   Ext: 2

REFERENCES

	page	lines
Mc. Lachlan (Ed) Portfolio for health (2)[1]: 'The developing programme of the DHSS in health service research' (1973) Nuffield Hospital Trust. Oxford University Press	45	10
Department of Health and Social Security, Welsh Office: 'Residential accommodation for mentally handicapped adults: local authority building Note 8' (1973) HMSO.	47	30
Hunter, H, Accreditation scheme for the handicapped' (13 January 1973) Health and Social Service Journal.	49	11

[1] *'Portfolio for health 2' includes Kushlick, A. 'Epidemiology and evaluation of services for the mentally handicapped and elderly' with bibliography. In a paper in the same volume: 'Mental health research' John Brothwood summarises a paper given by Dr Kushlick on the Wessex Survey of the mentally handicapped, and the register which was set up subsequently, as follows: 'From the register it was possible to select children for two hostels, one in Portsmouth and one in Southampton. The progress of the children in these hostels will be compared with others for whom it is not yet possible to provide hostel care. Within the hostels, factors which are considered to be anti-therapeutic are being identified. One of the major factors so far isolated has been staff shortages, which are particularly critical at certain times of the day'.*

References to the work done by the Session Editor, Dr Rosen, are also included in this volume.

ALTERNATIVES TO HOSPITAL AND HOSTEL CARE

Session Editor: Dr Maureen Hodgson, M B BS
Principal Medical Officer, Greater London Council. ILEA.

Alternatives to hospital (and hostel) care

A Training Officer, Oxford Regional Hospital Board (now Oxford AHA), opened the Information Exchange Session. He outlined the present position of those in hospitals for the mentally handicapped, who are awaiting release to community living. This in accord with the principles set out in: 'Better Services for the Mentally Handicapped'. HMSO. June 1971. He knew of about 300 patients (out of 500) that were ready for life in the community. They did not require hospital care. And yet it seemed it might take twenty or thirty years, as things stand at present, to provide alternative care for them. This he thought was cruel to the patients. Dr Cyril Williams (Consultant, Borocourt Hospital), had suggested that the local authority social services departments should be asked to take over all the hospital wards which now house mentally handicapped patients who do not require hospital treatment. Careful thought needed to be given to the kind of alternatives to hospital care local authorities intend to provide. In an unfriendly community hostels may not be the answer. They can easily become 'institutionalised' if not properly run. Patients cut off in the community came back to the hospital in the evening for their social life and entertainments. If 'lodgings' are provided, they only go to the 'high grades'. An experiment was described. Two elderly ladies who had been in Borocourt Hospital for about twenty years, were placed in a small Cheshire Group Home. They felt they could not fit in, and were glad to return again to their life in the hospital.

A participant, (City of Oxford) spoke about the need for avoiding competition between hospital and local authorities in seeking placement for the mentally handicapped in the community.

Home support services

It was the duty of social services departments to try to prevent the break-

59

down of family life for the mentally handicapped through effective home support services. Effective services would minimise the need to provide substitutes for family care. Most mentally handicapped children live at home (80%). With the exception of the small percentage who require continuous medical care in hospital, the main reasons for the remainder of the 20% not being at home does not seem to refer primarily to the degree of mental handicap or special care required.

The Session Editor pointed out that the prevention of breakdown of family life must start early, preferably when the handicap is first recognised. This might be at birth. In response to a suggestion that parents were 'not told' she had often heard this complaint but there were two points to consider. How should you tell parents and, second, how many parents will be able to accept the information that is given them? She gave an example of 'non-communication' with normal patients. Having given them the fullest information she found that when the patients passed this same information on to others, it was hardly recognisable as the information she had given them in the first place! 'One result of the way in which parents were informed is instantaneous rejection of the child. Another common attitude is rejection of the doctor who gives them the news.'

Substitutes for family life for those now living at home

Local authority social service departments

Foster care. A number of participants provided information on the development of foster care services, and there was considerable discussion of the problems involved. A Social Worker (London Borough of Merton) described her work in seeking supportive lodgings for the mentally handicapped and the mentally ill. The problem was finding suitable places. A Senior Social Worker (Northamptonshire), provided information on arrangements with which he was concerned in the Wellingborough area: two foster parents each take three children. A Senior Social Worker (Lewisham) described a Unit made up of eleven social workers (five full-time equivalent) which is now branching into mental handicap, but which normally deals with the placement for non-handicapped children. Three replies were received from an advertisement in the Nursing World; one mongol child was placed. A Principal Social Worker (Hackney) outlined some of the services provided for the mentally handicapped in the Borough. For full details of these see Mixing and Grouping (Page 29). The Assistant Information Officer, (Disabled Living Foundation), and a participant formerly with the Advisory Casework Service (MIND), reported enquiries they receive from social services departments for possible addresses for placements; there is an apparent need for some kind of central promotion of interest in fostering and supportive lodgings, with the possibility of listing names of those who may be prepared to offer places.

Rates for local authority payments to foster parents. Statistics were provided from NSMHC Information Archives on rates agreed between the London Boroughs; these were:— in 1972 0–4 years £4.80; 5–10 years £6.00; 11–14 years £7.20; 15–17 years £8.40.

The rates are inclusive of pocket money and clothing allowance: to be spent at the discretion of foster parents. They are for long-term foster care (over three months). For short-term foster care (under three months) deduct 50 pence. The rates are for normal children, and for handicapped children who do not present special difficulties due to their handicap (over and above the care needed for any child of that age). Foster parents caring for children who need special care due to their handicaps are entitled to rates up to double the rate for a normal child, although the maximum is very seldom paid. There is no recommended national scale. Each local authority determines its own rates depending upon the area and their own policy.

The rate for the job? There was a lively discussion on the part played by payment in encouraging foster care and a variety of views were expressed. It was suggested (by the Session Editor) that having regard to the high cost of residential care, say £30 to £40 per week (inc. capital outlay), higher rates might attract more foster-parents to apply. Several participants suggested that a higher quality of (possibly) trained foster-parents, who made a profession of their job, might emerge: others suggested that foster-parents, with a true vocation for their job, never even thought of asking how much they would be paid. On the other hand, it was also suggested that more permanence of placement is ensured, once foster parents come to rely upon the income they receive. The Guardianship Society had mentioned in correspondence that, in the lower income group foster families, the initial move to foster is frequently based upon financial reward, but that this initial motive can quickly change to a loving relationship, once the fostering situation is established.

The Guardianship Society. The Guardianship Society submitted brief written information which, at the request of participants, has been amplified, as follows:

'Subnormal persons admitted to the care of this Society are placed in foster homes of varying sizes according to their needs and they then either attend one of our training centres or if suitable are found part-time and in some cases full-time employment. They come to us from local authorities all over the country and are supervised by social visitors employed by the Society. Thus it is felt that they have the stability of a happy family background together with the stimulation and social training provided by the Centre, also opportunities for integration into the community. Many of those who come to us have been institutionalised for several years and now have the advantage of life in the outside world within their limitations. The Society also places a considerable number of subnormal men and women for holidays throughout the year which enables relatives, who care for them all the year round, a short period of relaxation.

It will be appreciated that for obvious reasons there are some types of patients for which we receive applications and which we are unable to place e.g. uncontrolled epileptics and mentally ill patients. Our limiting factor is the inability these days in finding sufficient foster homes to enable us to consider all the applications we receive. We feel that the changing services are suffering from teething troubles which is inevitable with a new organisation taking over.'

In response to a request for further information the Guardianship Society explained that they have had little success in finding foster homes through advertising and most new contacts come through their Social Visitors; three full-time and one part-time paid staff. Although the description of the work of this Society is included in this Report under 'Substitutes for family life for those now living at home', approximately half of their cases come from the parental home, via local authorities, and half are sent by the hospitals. The mentally handicapped under 16 years of age are no longer taken and fees vary (to the fostering families) from £8.40 to £17.50 (this where nursing care may be required). The average fostering fee would be from £9.45 to £10.50. The Guardianship Society, Grace Eyre Woodhead Memorial, Old Shoreham Road, Hove, BN3 6EW.

Supplement – or substitute? Over the last eight years there had been no referrals to hospital care by the City of Oxford. For the relief of parents, and where short-stay or extended care was required, this had been provided, not as a substitute, but as a supplement, to home life. The homes provided by the City of Oxford, both for children, and adults, are based on this principle.

Substitutes for family life for those now living in hospital

For those who are now resident in hospitals for the mentally handicapped it had been suggested at the opening of the Information Exchange Session that it might take twenty or thirty years – as things stand at present, to provide substitutes for family life for this institutionalised population of men, women and children. The problem which would take twenty to thirty years to solve was noted, briefly summarised from 'Better Services . . .', to be as follows:—

Twenty-five years ago, following the transfer of the old institutions to the hospital authorities when the National Health Service started (1948), local authorities ceased to provide residential care. As a substitute for family life the mentally handicapped were hospitalised, on social grounds, or occasionally on medical grounds.

Fourteen years ago, in an effort to remedy this situation, the Mental Health Act (1959) laid a duty on local authorities – ignored by the majority – to provide residential accommodation.

Two years ago, in a further effort to secure a remedy, '*Better Services . . .*' (1971) sanctioned the closing of hospital doors to those whose need was social. The *present position* is that backward local authorities now face two problems:—

PROBLEM ONE The need to provide residential accommodation for those no longer able to live at home – due, say, to the death of parents. This is the problem they solved in the past by hospitalisation.

PROBLEM TWO The need to provide residential accommodation for the return of those they put away, who are now being prepared by the hospitals (some 30,000) for return to their home communities.

It is the impact of these two problems, both of them new to the backward authorities, that it was suggested might take 20 or 30 years to solve. This crisis should not, however, overshadow the work of a few advanced local authorities who, as was shown by the contribution from Oxford, were well on the way to providing supplements, rather than substitutes, for family life, and were already, prior to the crisis, at an advanced stage of developing and refining them.

Progress in the rehabilitation of hospital patients. A Charge Nurse (South Ockendon Hospital) described the provision of prefabricated bungalows. Male and female patients live separately, but next door to each other, in groups of three. Six bungalows are already occupied by patients and a further six bungalows, when vacated by staff, will provide a total of 36 places. A participant pointed out, however, that hostels can easily become mini-hospitals.

The nurse as community worker. A Charge Nurse (Leytonstone Hospital) described her work in seeking placement in the community for suitable patients, in providing home visits to day patients, to patients boarded-out, and to patients living independently in the community. For this work the participant had been prepared by a Pilot Course (18

selected) run for Mental Subnormality Nurses by the North East Metro‐
politan Regional Hospital Board at the North Eastern Polytechnic
Stratford. See also special training courses for nurses described in 'Socia
Training and Social Competence.' (Page 71).

The contribution of the architect. A Consultant Architect (Centr
on Environment for the Handicapped) informed participants of the worl
currently undertaken by the Centre, and drew attention, in particular
to two recent publications.

Section 33. Mental Health Act. 1959

Statistics

The Session Editor suggested that statistics on fostering, supportive
lodgings, and guardianship (of the mentally handicapped) could be o
value to the Session participants. Statistics on fostering and supportive
lodgings separately classified for mentally handicapped children and
adults are not held centrally by the Department of Health and Socia
Security, although they may be available from some local authorities.

The following statistics were provided, upon request, for the Curren
Information Session, by Mr B. J. Hadkinson, DHSS

Numbers of mentally handicapped under guardianship: England only

	Admitted to Guardianship year ending 31. 3. 73	All under Guardianship (Mental Handicap)
TOTAL NUMBERS	26	158
Under Local Authority	25	138
Others	1	20
Male	16	81
Female	10	77
Aged Under 16 years	1	10
Aged 16 years +	25	148
Classification severely sub-normal	12	121
Classification sub-normal	14	37

Guardianship statistics are collected by the DHSS but they are no
published. This is mainly because, since classification of degree and kind

of handicap varies from local authority to local authority, and is not based on medical diagnosis, the reliability of the figures may be questioned.*

Placement under guardianship

Participants expressed surprise that the numbers of mentally handicapped covered by guardianship were so low. None of the participants had made use of Section 33, but it was thought that guardianship was intended to be linked with the provision of care (fostering or residential). That is, it would be the responsibility of a guardian to ensure that provision was made, and that needs were being met: it would not be the responsibility of the guardians to make the provision themselves. The Session Editor was of the opinion that there would be many people who would be prepared to say 'yes' to guardianship although they may say 'no' to providing foster care. The first was a responsibility, for which payment would not be expected. The second was a service, for which payment would be appropriate. It was noted that the powers conferred by Section 33 on a local authority, or with the approval of a local authority, upon an individual, are 'those which would be possessed by the guardian if the authority or the person concerned were the patient's father and the patient were under the age of fourteen'.

The NSMHC Trusteeship Scheme. It was noted, in concluding the Session, that the NSMHC have a nation-wide scheme, where they assume responsibility for all mentally handicapped persons – children or adults – whose parents wish, when they die, to have a watch kept upon the well-being of the surviving son or daughter. This is called a Trusteeship (not Guardianship) Scheme, although the general principle is that, wherever they may be, visitors will call at regular intervals. The Scheme is under a Board of Management appointed by the NSMHC (Chairman: Sir Noel Hutton). Responsibility has already been assumed for 47 mentally handicapped children and adults. The number of subscribers to the Scheme is now approaching 1000 parents (1973).

---

* See Information Exchange: 'Social Training and Social Competence.' (... serious consideration should be given to a more refined glossary of terms, and there is a need 'for ... genuine comparative data ...' (Page 78).

The Session Editor writes:

The task of this Session was a difficult one.

It set out to discuss possible solutions to the age-old problem of substitutes for the natural home, but excluded discussion of those solutions at present most popular; namely, hospitals and hostels.

This does not mean that we wished to shirk the responsibility but is explained by the fact that we felt each of the experiments and proposals outlined by the contributions required greater in-depth consideration; for example – fostering and guardianship – especially guardianship; one mainly undertaken by individual families, the other by 'authorities'.

Need this be so? Is there room for more voluntary work of the extended family kind? This in association with group homes and supportive lodgings? Cannot some of these homes and lodgings be adopted by groups in the community; businesses, societies, groups of individuals?

I would have liked to hear more about the South Ockendon work (See Page 63). Could the bungalows have been placed outside the hospital precincts – land being available? What factors turn a hostel into a mini-hospital? How is this prevented?

This was a very thought provoking day, indicating a need for many more 'get together and exchange information' Sessions.

Maureen Hodgson

Individual contributions are identified by page and line number on the List of Participants. References are identified by page and line, in the same way.

Participants Lists give the name, address, telephone number and post held at the time the contribution was made.

LIST OF PARTICIPANTS

SESSION EDITOR:

DR MAUREEN HODGSON, MB, BS   Principal Medical Officer,
Greater London Council, ILEA, The County Hall, SE1 7PB
Telephone: 01-633 5000

PARTICIPANTS

ARTHURTON, W.   Principal Social Worker, London Borough of   60   34–36
Hackney Social Services, 1 Hoxton Street, N1
Telephone: 01-986 3123   Ext: 6204

DEAKIN, MISS C.   Course Organiser, Counselling and Welfare,
NSMHC, 17 Pembridge Square, W2 4EP
Telephone: 01-229 8941

DOBSON, MISS H.   Secretary to the C.E.H., Centre on Environment for the Handicapped, 24 Nutford Place, W1H 6AN
Telephone: 01-262 2641

EVANS, N.   Senior Social Worker, Northamptonshire Social   60   26–28
Services Department, Croyland Hall, Wellingborough,
Northants
Telephone: 97 5614

HEPPER, MRS A.   Social Worker, Advisory Casework Services,   60–61   38– 4
National Association for Mental Health, 22 Harley Street,
London W1N 2ED
Telephone: 01-637 0741

LANE, MISS M.   Assistant Information Officer, Disabled Living   60–61   37– 4
Foundation, 346 Kensington High Street, London W14 8NS
Telephone: 01-602 2491

LAWRENCE, MRS L.   Senior Social Worker, Social Services Dept.,   60   28–34
London Borough of Lewisham, Eros House, Catford,
London SE6 4RU
Telephone: 01-690 4343

LUCK, J. H.   Training Officer, Oxford Regional Hospital Board,   59   1–22
Old Road, Headington, Oxford OX3 7LF
Telephone: Oxford 64861   Ext: 227

MARVELL, MRS J.   Charge Nurse, South Ockendon Hospital,   63   30–35
South Ockendon, Essex RM15 6SB
Telephone: 01-700 2335/7

MURPHY, MRS J.   Social Worker, Merton Social Services, 116   60   23–26
Kingston Road, London SW19
Telephone: 01-540 4475   Ext: 49

PARRINGTON, F.   Rehabilitation Officer, Bromham Hospital,   63   35–36
Near Bedford
Telephone: 023-02 2095

PURRETT, D. A.   Assistant Director of Social Services, (Residential   59–60   23– 7
and Day Care), City of Oxford Social Services Department,
George Street, Oxford, Oxford OX1 2BH   63   25–29
Telephone: Oxford 49811   Ext: 305

REFERENCES

	page	lines
INTERNATIONAL LEAGUE OF SOCIETIES FOR THE MENTALLY HANDI-CAPPED: 'Symposium on guardianship of the mentally retarded'[1] (1969) From NSMHC.	61	36
DINNAGE, R. and PRINGLE, M. L. 'Foster home care: facts and fallacies'[2] (1967) Longmans.	61	36
CLARKE, F. 'Hospital at home'[3] (9 June 1973) Health and Social Services Journal.	63	36
CENTRE ON ENVIRONMENT FOR THE HANDICAPPED: 'Handicapped people in ordinary houses and flats' (1973).	64	8
CENTRE ON ENVIRONMENT FOR THE HANDICAPPED: 'Improving existing hospital buildings for long stay residents' (1973).	64	8

[1] *Guardianship: The 'Symposium on guardianship' (above) defines the word 'guardianship' and its special application to the mentally handicapped, where decision making may be limited in specific areas. The definition given in this paper should not be confused with the word as it is used by the Guardianship Society: it should also not be confused with guardianship as provided for under the Mental Health Act which is dealt with in the appropriate section of these proceedings.*

[2] *Foster care. For a definition of the principles of foster care and the information available from research see: Dinnage, R. and Pringle, M. L. (above).*

[3] *Hospital at home: In her article Mrs Clarke describes a system, in Paris, of projecting hospital services into the community, in a pattern similar to pilot schemes in New York and Quebec. Primarily for the provision of medical care for patients who require hospitalisation, but who wish to stay at home, Mrs Clarke notes that this principle—of a hospital without walls—could have much wider application.*

SOCIAL TRAINING AND SOCIAL COMPETENCE

Session Editor: P W Jones Owen, BSc
Clinical Psychologist at Monyhull Hospital

Hospital Training Units and hostels
(under the National Health Service)

The Morning Session, attended by the Hon. Advisor to the Series, Dr Guy Wigley, provided a lively and generalised survey of participants' current activities.

Bromham Hospital. Of the 400 patients in the hospital, in ten wards, one ward unit of 50 beds has been arranged to provide a Training Unit for 41 patients age 18 to 58 years. The Gunzburg PAC Chart is used for progress assessment and activities are provided for broadly under self help, group living and community skills. A special feature of this Social Training Unit is that nursing staff, from ordinary wards, were given special training to adjust a nursing approach to a training approach, through a day release course (10 days spread over 10 weeks). The course was arranged by the Hertford Education Committee at Callowland Adult Education Centre, Watford (Mr H. E. Williams, Department of Adult Studies and Home Economics). Methods of selection and entrance requirements were described for a hostel in the community (staffed by the Hospital) to which the trained patients can transfer. In answer to a question from the Session Editor it was explained that the hostel was not a 'half-way' house where training was continued with a view to moving out to the community; it was a hostel designed to provide permanent care.

St Ebba's Hospital. This hospital was aiming at separating those patients considered 'pre-hostel' types, from those who will remain within the hospital for the rest of their lives. To this end it was hoped that the community within the hospital could be made equally satisfactory to the community outside. That is, having regard to the needs of the group selected, who would be unfitted to benefit from life in the open community.

71

At present 40 patients are in the pre-hostel group and are receiving training in work ability and self help. There were 220 trainees altogether and many were ready for community placement but provisions had not yet been made by the local authorities concerned.

Farleigh Hospital. Out of 200 beds, about 30% of patients, given adequate social training, may be able to take up hostel life in the community. An Aid to Daily Living Programme was described (See Page 74) and the development of a 'half-way house' (hostel); this at present houses 4 females and 2 males.

St Lawrence's Hospital. At this 1,800 bed hospital patients are assessed at ward level prior to social training, first on a trial basis. Progress assessment is made according to a scheme which is very effective in showing what they cannot do and the kind of help they will need in certain situations; this, with a view to the patients travelling outside of the hospital or of taking up residence in one of three hostels set either within the hospital grounds, in a nearby village, or in Croydon (the nearest town).

Permanent hostel care. Dr Guy Wigley, before departing from the Morning Session, took up the point raised by the provision of a hostel at Bromham Hospital for permanent care. The Session Editor had questioned whether this hostel was in fact a suitable solution. Should not residents in this hostel have the opportunity to move on to other forms of living? What is the definition of a 'hostel'. What was a hostel for? Would the answer to this question depend upon the way it was used?

Dr Wigley described his use of guardianship schemes; at one time, he was aware of at least 100 adults being cared for in this way. He felt that the possibility of fostering and guardianship had not been fully explored. A social worker charged with seeking suitable homes for mentally handicapped people had regarded 5 placements in three months as a 'terrible failure'. But 5 placements in three months was 20 in a year! The complete population of a medium hostel!

Dr Wigley felt it was essential that proper psychological testing was applied to potential foster care placements, with special regard to the tolerance levels of the fostering parties concerned. Wrong placement could be wasteful of efforts and could impair the goodwill of both fostering families and the public. He also referred to the danger of crude guesses with regard to placement in work, and in the community setting. The process of how to move from A to B must be controlled and for this the advice of the psychologist can be of value. There was, above all, a need for continuing assessment and one individual social worker to act in a supportive role. Foster placement, without these supportive services, may lead to failure and recrimination.

Discussion. It was suggested that it was not possible to measure 'potential'. However, data had been analysed from a Scissor Test (designed by the London Borough of Croydon) which had shown that 80% predictability could be achieved with it, but that personality and emotional factors were also important. O'Connor suggests, having regard to a group specified by him, that it is advisable to provide for a trial, rather than to select or exclude, on the basis of tests.

In local authority adult training centres and hostels (under directors of social service)

Balmoral Adult Training Centre (Hertfordshire County Council). This Centre has 120 trainees of which 10 are physically handicapped. The outwork (contract work) done by the Centre has to be viable but was selected not only with regard to profitability, but also with respect to instructional value. The Centre runs for 25 hours a week of which 2 hours were originally devoted mainly to domestic science, reading, writing and arithmetic. However, following attendance at a NSMHC Regional Conference at Exeter, a scheme for assessment of social competence was introduced, designed to identify the minimum skills required for living in the community. The Centre were not 'sold' on the use of Progress Assessment Charts. For trainees aged 17 to 21 years the method was a waste of time, although clearly valuable for the mentally handicapped under the age of 16 years. A simple scheme for the evaluation of social competence was used which covered personal hygiene, manners, perceptual ability and word recognition. Progress made was checked regularly but it was necessary to concentrate on practical essentials. This was clearly necessary when 35% of trainees could not clean their nails and 55% were not able to distinguish between male and female toilets, with consequent problems. Close co-operation with parents was important in developing a trainee's social competence. The present organisation of the Social Services Department was such that the Deputy Director responsible for adult training provisions was not the same person as the Deputy Director responsible for field social work. Social workers did not like training centre staff crossing into the threshold of the parental home. Parents come to the Manager – the Manager cannot go to the parents.

It is not the value of social education for the 16+ group that is being questioned here, but the value of directed social education based upon the use of the Gunzburg Progress Assessment Charts. Directed social training can in fact achieve very substantial results with this age group: 'The highest increase by an individual trainee was from 7.7 to 14.1, a rise of 6.4 years in social age. The two next highest results were from 10.8 to

14.4 and from 7.7 to 11.3, an increase of 3.6 years in social age in each case'.

Social Services: London Borough of Westminster. A wide-ranging review of the socialisation services for the mentally handicapped was given for this London Borough, and the uses made of evening school facilities, Salvation Army and Gateway Clubs, holiday projects, cycle maintenance courses, and similar facilities.

A recent survey, of special interest from the social training point of view, had been undertaken to determine the policy followed by local authorities in the payment of incentive allowances at training centres. These seemed to vary very considerably, being based on work output and good attendance, from 10p a week to £2.00 a week (£1.50 average). Incentives were socially important and they should be more consistent.

It was here noted that attempts to maintain some degree of independence are discouraged, even penalised; for example, a cripple who wishes to augment his income by working finds that as soon as this exceeds £2.05 (in 1970) his social security benefit is correspondingly cut.

Also, whilst, the severely subnormal are probably less influenced by long-term goals, it has been shown that the mentally handicapped do respond in a normal way to incentives. An experimental study with the severely subnormal on motivation and performance showed that incentives have an enormous effect, greatly increasing the performance of groups given goal incentives (score 258) as compared with those given encouragement (score 125). The control group who were simply given instructions scored only 86 to 101. Dr Wigley, however, pointed out the danger of trainees becoming fixed in trivial work tasks if careful assessment and follow-up is not maintained. Performance, and response to incentives deteriorates if the tasks are tedious and devoid of interest.

Brian Didsbury Training Centre (London Borough of Newham). A description was given of the use of an Aids to Daily Living Programme. A detail from the ADL Programme (given as an example) included nine questions on opening containers and ten questions on other kinds of vessels, using a variety of can openers and methods. Also a report was given on the liaison between Training Centre and Hostel; good support from the Community Psychologist, close co-operation with the Social Services Department, regular staff meetings, and a generally co-operative and go-ahead model of social development for the mentally handicapped. Dr Wigley, having regard to his earlier links with the London Borough of Newham, said that his heart was warmed by the description given of the recent advances made there.

Group social services (Mid-Essex). Here a 'minimal Support Unit' was described, (two council houses made into one house) which serves as a 'satellite' to an Adult Hostel, where individuals are prepared to live under minimum support conditions. Supervision is provided for the Unit by staff from the adult hostel.

The Folkestone Training Centre (Kent County Council). A hostel and training centre are provided in a single building accommodating (in training) 90 trainees age over 16 years (mentally and physically handicapped). Of particular interest was the use made of the College of Further Education for word recognition, art, reading and writing. Also, mainly due to the profitability of contract work, a special activities programme has been developed for those severely subnormal who are unlikely to take up work in sheltered or open employment. This programme includes dancing lessons, netball, football and similar activities. It had been suggested that research might be of value to establish the most effective kind of programme for the non-employable, non-work group of the mentally handicapped.

The Brixton Adult Training Centre (London Borough of Brixton). This, it was reported was an architect's dream! There were 150 trainees to 15 staff (3 senior instructors and 12 assistant instructors). A classroom is provided for social training and social education for which further extensive facilities are provided. These include a fully fitted flat for training in domestic life and independence (planning of meal, shopping, use of money and public transport). A self service dining-room is provided. No report was made on the extent to which directed social training and progress assessment was used. The Session Editor questioned where the responsibility lay, in a local authority, for relating the architect's design of – say – an adult training centre to its role and aims. He thought that it was important that any environment for the mentally handicapped should be carefully matched to its purpose, and that the aim of the social training given should also be arranged to correspond to the end in view.

Discussion. Concern was expressed about the effectiveness of co-operation within the social services: some social workers object to involvement with parents of the mentally handicapped, and are reluctant to bring all parties together: this led to problems of keeping cases continually under review so that all the facts on social competence and skills are readily available. It was suggested that parent participation could be of value at Pembridge Information Exchange Sessions. The Secretary reported that parents did attend and the Sessions had been well publicised to parents through the NSMHC Journal 'Parents Voice'. It was possible that parents found attendance difficult unless Sessions could be held in the evenings or at weekends, as is normal with most NSMHC meetings involving parents.

Schools (under Department of Education and Science)

In order to limit the present Series of Information Exchanges to reasonable numbers representatives from special schools had not been invited to the current Session. Several participants, however, had noted the value of social education for those under sixteen years, and also for those now remaining in school beyond this age (16/19 years).

Attention was drawn to the possibility of mixing the physically handicapped and the mentally handicapped. For treatment of this topic, see Page 25. It was also noted that some form of social training was required for pupils at special schools who tend to be cut off from every day life: they do not know what is socially acceptable. Dr Wigley described the advances being made by the Inner London Education Authority in ensuring that social workers visit all day schools for the handicapped – including the mentally handicapped. They hope in this way to secure adequate communication with all the agencies concerned including, parents.

The use and misuse of 'labelling'

In closing the Information Session the Session Editor, in reply to a question concerning the use of the Vineland Social Maturity Scale said that the weakness of Doll's work was that this scale was based on a comparison of mentally handicapped with normal people, and not of the mentally handicapped with each other, according to their average capacities. Scales of measurement suitable for use with mentally handicapped have, in the past, been related to standards of normality. The Vineland Scale was designed for use in America, not in England.

Whilst many examples of mixing and grouping the mentally handicapped had been given, (Page 25), little was said of the theory or aim which – long term – lay behind these methods. Was some mixing and grouping simply a response to the limits set by the present inadequate provisions.

The Session Editor said hostels, hospitals and training centres could either provide 'storage', or they could provide directed training and treatment. For example, if hostels were to be seen as places where individual treatment was given, (rather than simple caring) then measurement of progress, diagnosis of specific areas of need, and appropriate remedial action are required. Without such measurement and diagnosis (of social competence) the mentally handicapped will continue to be regarded, both by staff and public, with a generic (them and us) attitude. Hospital patients being returned to the community were creating a problem of crisis proportions: was this to some extent due to lack of proper measurement (and treatment) of social competence prior to discharge to the community? (Page 83)

Finding out what can be measured in a repeatable way, and relating the measurement of one variable to another, is part of the work of psychology. Because much of the literature appears to be written in a complex style (to meet the disciplines of research) some participants had given the impression that the contributions of psychology had little of practical utility value to offer staff in their day to day work with the retarded.

The Session Editor explained that the aim of the Progress Assessment Chart, (which he handed to participants for examination) was in fact to transform psychological measurements, (based on intensive studies), into simple tools that could be used with a minimum of error by staff who have no need for special qualification in using them.[1]

The second point, an apparent resistance to 'labelling' the mentally handicapped into 'categories', (through testing) also seemed to be based on a misunderstanding. The aim was not to label the persons but to label the need. The Editor reminded participants that we have an education system which theoretically classifies and segregates by age, by need, and by ability, simply in order that – at the output – there shall be a chance given to each individual to make the most advantage of their individual capacities according to the opportunity open to them. Classification for opportunity – not classification for life – is the aim.

---

[1] *Since the NSMHC Slough Project (1964)—see Baranyay (ibid.), most training courses for professional staff now include social training.*

See: 'Organisation and contents of a one year course leading to Diploma in the training and further education of mentally handicapped adults'. Training Council for Teachers of the Mentally Handicapped (1972) Department of Health and Social Security, London. See section: 'Teaching Social Competence'. In order to select priorities for teaching and training the student will need to assess each trainee's needs, and determine realistic objectives in the light of his degree of handicap and his probable future mode of living.

'Model of good practice: local authority training centres for mentally handicapped adults' (1968) Department of Health and Social Security, London. States that: 'The team should include . . . trained staff able to give instruction . . . in social skills . . .'.

'List of Approved Courses leading to (a) Diploma of the Council and (b) Manager's Course (Adult training centres)' Training Council for Teachers of the Mentally Handicapped. Published annually. Department of Health and Social Security, London.

77

The Session Editor writes :

May I say how delighted I was with the outcome of the Informatio Exchange Session.

All preconceived ideas which I harboured were swiftly dispelled by th end of the day. It is only when we as individuals actively participate i such discussions that one realises how often we talk at cross purpose.

It was generally felt that the study of – and treatment within – sub normality had reached a stage which required genuine comparative dat as the basis for future rehabilitation. Many of the participants expresse the feeling that serious consideration should be given to a more refine 'glossary of terms' within the field.

I personally hope that the trend away from the restricted and isolate environments of the past should not in the future lead to a 'hotch potch of different standards from one local authority to another. It is eviden that much work remains to establish criteria of basic minimum require ments for hostels, group homes etc. in terms of the physical environmen More important still perhaps is the recognition that such criteria b considered by the various authorities, whose task it is to establish suc dwellings.

Many thanks to all those present for a most informative day and fo their support which made my task a pleasant one.

P. W. Jones Owe

Individual contributions are identified by page and line numbe on the List of Participants. References are identified by pag and line, in the same way.

Participants Lists give the name, address, telephone number an post held at the time the contribution was made.

LIST OF PARTICIPANTS

SESSION EDITOR:
JONES OWEN, P. W., BSC   Clinical Psychologist, Monyhull Hospital,
Monyhull Hall Road, Birmingham, B30 3QB
Telephone: 021-444 2271

PARTICIPANTS

REFERENCES

	page	lines
O'Connor, N. and Tizard, J. 'The social problem of mental deficiency' (1956) Pergamon London (See chapter: 'The prediction of occupational success').	74	21
Baranyay, E. P. 'The mentally handicapped adolescent' (1971) Pergamon Press.	74	2
Miller, E. J. and Gwynne, G. V. 'A life apart' (1972) Tavistock Publications. J. B. Lippincott Company.	74	13
Skandinaviska Tesforlaget A.B. 'Vilunda scheme 1 to 3' (For PRE-ADL work) Sturegatan. 56-114/36 Stockholm.	74	31
Liljeroth and Nimeus. 'Primar ADL training handlening'. (For ADL Programme).	74	31
Gunzburg, H. and Gunzburg, A. 'Mental handicap and physical environment' (1973) Bailliere Tindall.	75	28
Marshall, A. 'The abilities and attainments of children leaving junior training centres' (1967) The National Association for Mental Health (MIND).	76	23

RETURN TO COMMUNITY LIFE

Session Editor: Elizabeth Marais

Head Teacher, Kevill-Davies School, Little Plumstead Hospital;
Member of the Executive of the National Federation of Gateway Clubs

Return to community life

The plight of men and women who are returned from institutional life to the community had recently been described in the following terms:—

A discharged patient is poorly equipped to meet the demands and pressures outside hospital. He is expected to manage his own financial affairs, including income tax returns, national insurance, supplementary benefits, savings and rent. He must cope with an unaccustomed variety of relationships: landlady, tradesmen, the foreman, workmates, the chap next door, girl friends and so on. As a hospital patient, he has not been required to think much for himself. There has always been the charge nurse to advise and direct him, tell him when to get up, go to work, bath, shave, change his clothes, visit dentist, doctor or optician. Outside he is hit by his own inability to deal with such matters unaided. He is alarmed to discover so many essential tasks that he must accomplish if he is to function, at the simplest level, in what appears to be a very complex society.

Examples of pre-crisis situations (and crisis situations) had also been given:

Jean. Jean engages in casual prostitution. On leaving hospital she was neat, well-groomed and had been taught to take an interest in her appearance. In spite of all efforts to help her, she has become sluttish, despondent and lacking in initiative to improve her condition. The social worker who visits feels she should have remained in hospital until a hostel was available for her.

Simon, George and Jerry. Simon, George and Jerry are on probation for alleged sexual offences against minors . . . . All were apparently encouraged in these acts by younger boys who were

83

mentally more mature, but technically juvenile. The offenders, although mentally immature, were adults and therefore held to be responsible. A young man discharged from a subnormality hospital is especially vulnerable because, lacking insight and perceptiveness, he is often naively unaware that much of his instinctive behaviour is socially unacceptable. Having lived in an all-male ward, the chances are that he will have had some homosexual encounters. In addition, his mental immaturity will lead him to go around with younger boys. This can create an explosive situation, which may soon bring him into conflict with the law. Even if relationships are innocent, any kind of horse-play is liable to misinterpretation.

Lester. Lester has been discharged for almost five years, after 25 years as a patient. At first he was employed as a corporation gardener, but proved to be a slow worker and has now been unemployed for three years. He is married to a mentally handicapped girl and they have an 18 month old son. The couple argue a great deal, but their relationship has improved since they moved away from his wife's mother (also mentally retarded) . . . . A social worker sees the family as often as possible but admits that his case-load is too heavy to give the regular support they need.

Joe and Mary. Joe and Mary, both in their mid-twenties, are living together. Their sense of responsibility towards each other, and to the community, has noticeably deteriorated. Domestic strife has worsened since another retarded lad joined the household. Complaints from neighbours are frequent as squabbles within the house increase.

John. John, in his mid-forties, was in hospital for 20 years. Now he works as a hotel kitchen porter and lives in lodgings. He has frequent disagreements with his landlady . . . . He needs constant reminding about shaving regularly, keeping himself clean and wearing his artificial teeth. John is only just coping; he looks painfully thin and admits to not eating regularly. He does not manage his money well and has hire-purchase commitments which he has difficulty in maintaining. He has had one or two visits from the local authority social worker, but neither remembers the latter's name nor how to contact him.

This study concludes with the following comment:—

Unless greater priority is given to the plight of the mentally handicapped, the problem may reach crisis proportions. We might then have to decide if we are being more humane than our predecessors, who shut away their 'defectives'.

We may be treating them less well. Casting the mentally handicapped adrift in the cities, without help, is more destructive than putting them away.

Examples of supportive services

The Royal Earlswood Hospital. Following the Mental Health Act, 1959, when all patients, except those on court order, were given voluntary status, many of the higher grade patients at the Royal Earlswood were placed in the community. Following the Government White Paper (HMSO 1971) the hospital had expanded their services for the rehabilitation of the lower-grade patients, with a view to them taking up life in the community setting. A Management Study was undertaken to investigate community rehabilitation with particular reference to liaison with local authority social workers and social services, with a view to making recommendations. Arrangements were made by the hospital to rent a house on a new council estate. Liaison in these arrangements were facilitated by the County Medical Officer concerned being also a member of the Hospital Management Committee. Four male patients have been placed in the house and all have been found local employment. The residents on the council estate were not informed of the arrangements made. Arrangements were made to alert the churches, local associations, women's guilds, and local employment offices. The house is situated $12\frac{1}{2}$ miles from the hospital, so that residents may call back to the hospital in the evenings, should they wish to do so.

   Cost of project. The weekly expenditure (four residents) for 1973/74 was:—

Item	£ p
Rent	5.23
Nursing Assistant (Part-time)	8.00
Food	12.00
Milk	1.00
Nursing Officer (Visits)	2.40
Transport	1.25
Bread	0.30
Laundry	0.30
Surrey County Council	3.00
Transport (Goods Delivery)	1.50
Cleaning: Sundries	0.50
Fuel (Heating and Lighting)	2.00
Telephone	0.50
	37.98

The above breakdown shows a cost per resident per week of a little under £10.00. Since each resident contributes £6.00 from earnings, the net running cost is therefore £4.00 per resident per week. In practice, for hospital accounting purposes, the cost of the project (£37.98 per week) also took into account the normal cost per patient per week (in hospital), which, in 1973/74, was £28.55 times four = £114.20. The £6.00 contributed by each resident (£24.00 per week) was then paid in as income to the hospital central account.

Examples were given of the value of this kind of minimal support unit in anticipating and preventing crisis. The Project has been running for a year. One patient was seen to deteriorate and his financial affairs had to be entirely looked after by staff. He was taken back to the hospital and was replaced by another patient. One resident encountered trouble in open employment where it appeared, on outdoor work, that he suffered urinary incontinence. After careful investigation it was found that this patient had originally been institutionalised for indecent exposure, and was therefore in fear of seeking normal relief. Having traced this problem it was possible to re-settle this resident in employment where ordinary toilets were available. The desire of the residents to undertake the hire-purchase of a colour television might have lead to trouble but it was possible to alert the rental firm to the legal issues involved, and a satis-factory arrangement was made. The residents (all four of them) now deliver their weekly payments (a bag of mixed change) each Saturday morning, at the local offices of the rental firm. This project may be compared with the Minimal Support Unit described earlier. (Page 74.) Briefly, this comprised two council houses made into one house, which served as a 'satellite' to an Adult Hostel. Here, individuals are prepared to live under minimum support conditions. Supervision is pro-vided for the Unit by staff from the local Adult Hostel.

Co-operation with Social Services Department. The figure shown in the breakdown of expenditure (above) includes an amount to Surrey County Council, covering the provision by the local authority of what was originally 6 hours a week but has now been changed to include the cooking of an evening meal for the residents upon their return from work (15 hours a week). The amount shown for the nursing assistant covered the provision of initial support by a paid volunteer awaiting university entrance, for the first 6 months, to encourage the residents initiative in handling the management of the house (gas, electricity, laundry, cooking, cleaning, maintenance, etc.). Personal visits to the Project from the hospital, were made once each week. It was suggested that 'minimal support' projects could also be run effectively in ordinary residential housing situations.

Discussion. It was suggested, with regard to the Royal Earlswood Minimal Support Project (described above) that to not inform the local community prior to a development of this kind was unethical. It was explained that this was a special case. The house had never before been occupied, and it was on a new estate where, as the new tenants arrived, it would be they who needed to adjust to the neighbourhood situation. It was also explained that, whilst it might appear unethical to not inform local residents, the powers that make such informing action necessary would depend upon the particular circumstances; for example, should planning permission (for new hostels) or change of use permits (for the modification of existing buildings) prove necessary.

St Ebba's Hospital. Work was being done here to bridge the gap between institutional care and life in the community; this also included the work done in bringing the community into the hospital, the tracing of 'lost' parents and relatives, work with pre-hostel groups, and the securing of outside employment for patients. Male patients, after training, are placed in adult hostels in Roehampton and Mitcham. Female patients may be placed in South Side Home Streatham (for pre-hostel training) and The Turret, a hostel providing residential facilities for 16 girls in single rooms, who all enjoy open employment. A number of patients who had been discharged in the community, return regularly to enjoy their holidays in the hospital setting. A recently converted isolation ward is now used as a Self-Care Unit. It provides accommodation for patients who are able to take full responsibility for themselves. These patients, whilst they would be competent for community care, did not wish to leave the hospital.

Leavesden Hospital. A unit within the hospital, linked to a community hostel (in Watford) belonging to the hospital services was described. Provided within the hospital is a 14-bedded Unit with one enrolled nurse (night-duty), plus two occupational therapists who attend the Unit 5 days a week from 9 to 4 o'clock. This Unit is for female patients awaiting community hostel placements, and ten of the fourteen receive social training whilst four go out of the hospital to daily employment. Training usually lasts for about three months and out of 130 patients who have taken the course, about 70 to 80 have gone out of the hospital.

At the community hostel run by the hospital services the ten under training are arranged in three groups; shopping, cooking, housework and cleaning. The groups change their tasks each week. There are four social workers in the hospital and visits are made to patients placed in the community and employers. Placements have been made in residential employment, a few have gone back to their parental homes and some have gone to local authority hostels; use is also made of the Watford Hostel (described below). Twelve beds are provided in four bedrooms. All residents are female. Residents are given social training, and are taught home-care, self-care, and self-discipline. Thirty-eight girls have now left the hostel permanently for community life. This number includes one placed in an old persons' home, one married, four to residential employment (two of these failed), one to a Self-Care Unit at Manor Hospital, three to their own bed-sits, and six have discharged themselves; ten have left permanently for various local authority areas. At present there are eleven residents in the Hostel. One awaits a bed-sit, one a special home for the deaf and dumb, and five are ready and awaiting local authority hostel placement. Eight of the residents attend cookery classes at Cassio Adult Training College, Watford, one evening a week. Ten residents were returned to hospital. For these patients a further effort is made in rehabilitation by the hospital, and patients are then given further trials as hostel residents. The experience of hostel life is a little less of a shock to them on each subsequent occasion.

Under the social services. A hostel was described, in Maidenhead, run by the Berkshire Social Services Department which provides 26 places. There are at present six care staff; the Superintendent and Matron, two Deputies, and two Care Assistants. About half the residents have been admitted from hospitals (several), and about half the residents have been admitted from the community.

The work of local authority social service departments

Oxfordshire. An urban area and villages (population about 50,000) with Bicester at its centre was described. In this area there were no hospitals for the mentally handicapped; no hostels and no training centres. The nearest provisions of this kind were training centres for adults at Banbury, Witney and Wheatley; one adult hostel at Witney and one hostel for children at Banbury. There are hospitals for the mentally handicapped at Burford and Reading. A review had been undertaken into the needs of parents with mentally handicapped members living at home. When this survey was done, (about a year ago) half of these cases were 'ticking-over' with the aid of family support, and given more staff and finance, about half of them would possibly benefit with more support from social services. So far as mentally handicapped children are concerned, parents with children under five require substantial support. Once they settled in school, the family situation becomes quiescent until young adulthood, when special needs then arise and have to be met.

Cambridgeshire and Isle of Ely. A case was described of a young man who was given two years prison sentence for sexual offences and bestiality; this sentence was changed to treatment in a hospital for the mentally handicapped. Upon release from hospital his parents wanted him back home but in the village where they lived there was great antagonism about his return. Arrangements were then made for the family to be transferred to a council house in a new community where the young man would not be known. The young man is now living with his sister on a farm and is self-supporting. With a case load of eighty, of which twenty were cases of mental handicap, it was thought the apparent high incidence was due to 'in-breeding'. Six cases had been returned from hospital to the community. Some went back to near relatives, but this will frequently depend upon why they went into hospital in the first place, and providing that the family situation is not impossible. Some residential hotel employment has been found, but this tends to break down. A new adult hostel is due to open in the near future.

East Sussex. Provisions in Hove were outlined. For mental health, a specialist social worker was now employed. A 'boarding-out' scheme was under development, also the use of family aids, as visitors to families in need of support.

Southampton. A social worker was attached to Tatchbury Mount Hospital, (600 patients; one villa for children; the rest adults). His 'role' to date was to establish good relationships between the local authority and the hospital services. The rate of discharge from hospital to community had been low. This was to some extent due to the reluctance of the hospital to discharge superior patients, and the need to improve the transfer structure. Several patients are on local authority waiting lists and two have been placed in residential employment in hotels. Arrangements have been made for hospital patients to attend an adult training centre in the community, as a stepping-stone towards community return. Some of the 25 beds provided by an adult hostel in Southampton have been offered to the hospital for patients ready for a supported life in the community setting.

Beyond crisis intervention

Contributors discussed the information that had been exchanged during the Morning Session and the Session Editor asked participants whose responsibility they thought it was to deal with crisis situations when they arise in the community. What button should be pressed in an emergency, and by whom? She reminded participants of the examples of crisis given in her paper, and said that currently she was aware of fifteen problem cases where the individuals concerned did not even know the name of their local authority social worker: these people moved from crisis to crisis. She had, herself, at a recent weekend, tried to deal with an emergency which had resulted in sixteen telephone calls having to be made. In this particular case, when a local authority social worker who knew of the case was eventually contacted, he said that nothing useful could be done. He said the case was long-term, was intractable, that the individual concerned was not helpful, of low IQ, and that the case was not viable. It appeared to the Session Editor that the social worker was evaluating this case as if it were that of a person of normal intelligence, who was himself responsible for the crisis he was in.

Danger of facile and over-sentimental approach. It was also recognised that the subnormal has a general vulnerability, and not the wit to call for help; also, that it sometimes appears that there are not enough social workers or home helps available to allow them to have the life in the community which they all deserve. It would however, be quite wrong for social workers to be carried away by a facile and over-sentimental approach. Clearly many subnormal require a continuing programme of support and training. Social Service Departments can deal with short-term crisis, and also long-term crisis where a situation is tractable. It would be wrong to think, so far as the social worker was concerned, that compared with the crisis relief needed by others, the subnormal present a special case. All of us have a right to be looked after when we are vulnerable, in old age, grief and sickness. The continuing supportive care and training of the subnormal, and the anticipation of crisis, was not a matter for the social worker in the social services department. Certainly, in one case quoted by the Session Editor, where emergency accommodation was required for a mentally handicapped couple, the social service department should, and could, have made provision for this.

Discovering, anticipating and preventing crisis. The Session Editor quoted a case where, following an emergency, a young man had said to her 'I reckon I was better off in hospital'. She pointed out that there was no hostel for the mentally handicapped in her area and that returned hospital patients were placed directly in the community. They made use of the Wednesday Club for the Mentally Handicapped (Affiliated to the National Federation of Gateway Clubs). This club met only one night a week and was staffed by volunteers. She felt it might be possible that, in areas without special provision for those who return to community life, the Gateway Clubs do provide a means of keeping in touch with patients and anticipating problems. It is not possible, however, for the clubs to manage the problems. They are without trained staff, and without the money required to support social work.

The National Federation of Gateway Clubs. This Federation was set up in 1966 and now has over 300 affiliate clubs (15 inside hospitals). Although the primary aim of these clubs is to provide lesisure for the mentally handicapped, as a 'spin-off' club leaders can also keep an eye on those members who are known to have been discharged from hospital. Dirty clothes, trouble with neighbours, and other problems can be anticipated before trouble becomes serious. The clubs also have the advantage that there is a happy informal atmosphere, so that mentally handicapped people do not feel they are being visited by Big Brother. Many clubs have also forged links with the social service departments in their area, so that expert advice can be sought when needed. A particular example was given of a young man (in Leeds) who, due to the training received before discharge from hospital, was able to look after his flat, was liked by his neighbours, and managed to settle in the community. Then he bought himself a dog. He was unable to train, control, and look after the dog. This led to a critical situation in the neighbourhood, and drew attention to the young man's degree of handicap. A Club Leader was able to resolve this problem by helping the club member, and also the dog, to adjust! The Session Editor had described, in the case of Lester and his wife, the work of young helpers from the club, who assisted the wife with the child, provided baby clothes, food parcels and occasional baby sitting: this last was started when it was discovered that the child was being left unattended for long periods. In the cases of Simon, George and Jerry, on probation for alleged sexual offences against minors, the club had paid for a solicitor to defend each of them.

Discussion. It was suggested that the decision whether this or that person is able to take his place in the community should be made by a Medical Officer. The Honorary Advisor to the Series of Information Exchanges, Dr Guy Wigley, during an earlier Session, had pointed to 'the danger of crude guesses with regard to placement in work, and in the community setting. The process of how to move from A to B must be controlled and for this the advice of the psychologist can be of value. There was, above all, a need for continuing assessment and for one individual social worker to act in a supportive role. Community placement, without these supportive services, may lead to failure and recrimination'. With regard to the fifteen people who were supposed to be 'independent' (to which the Session Editor had referred) the decision to place them in the community must have been made either because they were thought likely to succeed without specialist support, or because it was thought they should be given the opportunity for learning to succeed in the community. Had these decisions been properly made? The Session Editor had mentioned that hospital social workers had in most cases been responsible for the community placements made. It was pointed out, however, that, even in the hostel situation, it was often difficult to anticipate crises. Many hostels admitted the mentally ill, the subnormal, the severely-subnormal and the psychotic. At the Maidenhead Hostel (Page 88) about half the admissions came from the community and about half from hospitals. Those admitted from hospitals were referred to hospital social workers: those admitted from the community were referred to local authority social workers. Records that came with the patients were unreliable. They did not disclose the whole story. They did not know the background to the admissions and did not know what to expect. A case was cited of a psychotic highly-disturbed young woman admitted from her parental home in the community. Her parents were much involved. She was thought by the hospital psychologist to be a hostel case but was violent and difficult to manage. She went into the town and was raped. Two young men residents went into the town and sexually assaulted a boy. It was not possible from these patients' records to anticipate these problems as they had not known the residents prior to the admission to the hostel. The attitude of the neighbourhood to the hostel had deteriorated since the first residents had arrived (in April 1973). Her own child now had no other children to play with: neighbours would not allow their own children to play in the hostel grounds, although her own child was often invited out to play in the houses of other children. It was suggested that the proper organisation of voluntary services, (by the Social Services Departments) in accord with the Aves Report, could possibly provide a positive scheme for supportive services. The Session Editor had referred in her article to young married couples now out of hospital who have either unwanted children, or children who have to be taken into care because they cannot manage them. Referral for sex education and birth control advice could possibly be supervised through co-ordinated voluntary helpers, i.e. wvs, Red Cross and similar organisations.

The Session Editor said, in closing the Session, that it was her impression that returned hospital patients are placed much more easily in the villages and small towns, rather than in large cities (for example, Norwich). Quoting McCulloch, she said: 'What constitutes subnormality is to a very large extent socially determined by the threshold of community tolerance.'

The Session Editor writes:

This Information Exchange Session highlighted the fact that there is a great deal of good-will and many people committed to the welfare of the mentally handicapped, but all too often they find themselves working in isolation with no clearly defined line of communication. It is regrettable that we do not appear to utilise this good-will more effectively by achieving better co-operation and liaison between all organisations and people, professional and voluntary, who are involved in the task of helping discharged hospital patients to adapt to life in the community.

No one doubted that mentally handicapped individuals should be discharged from hospital whenever possible, but what happens next is all too often left to chance. In some areas there is undoubtedly good and constant liaison between hospital staff and local authority social workers, areas where adequate hostels provide that vital half-way stage between the dependence of hospital life and the total independence of life in the community. Unfortunately there is evidence that liaison is not always in existence, and in many cases social workers are not made aware of hospital patients discharged into their area because it is assumed that upon discharge the patient becomes an independent citizen able to manage his own affairs. Our discussion revealed that the people who learn of the plight of many former patients reaching crisis situations in the community are those responsible for the day to day care in hostels and those running clubs for the handicapped. Yet these are the people who are supplied with very scanty information about the cases they are concerned with and who seldom have the power or the resources to either provide the help needed or summon assistance from the appropriate sources.

Voluntary workers, especially those working in Gateway Clubs, obviously play a vital part in befriending and helping the mentally handicapped, but often they are ill-equipped to offer the counselling services needed.

The cut back in social services expenditure means that there are too few social workers and too little money available to provide the supportive help needed for men and women discharged from subnormality hospitals. However, the fact that many of these unfortunates are finding their way into Gateway Clubs should not be overlooked. Here, surely, is the point of contact where the professional social worker can give active support advising the Leader and voluntary workers and perhaps visiting a club regularly to set aside a time and place within the club to provide a counselling service.

The two questions, 'When does a person cease to be dependent and become independent?' and 'Who decides?' were not really answered satisfactorily. Could it be that we must accept that some individuals require supportive help of one kind or another all their lives and that we, who are more fortunate, should be prepared to go on propping them up even if, in the words of one social worker, they are unco-operative, intractable and will never learn to keep out of trouble?

Can we really dismiss this as mere sentimentality?

Elizabeth Marais

Individual contributions are identified by page and line number on the List of Participants. References are identified by page and line, in the same way.

Participants Lists give the name, address, telephone number and post held at the time the contribution was made.

LIST OF PARTICIPANTS

SESSION EDITOR:

MARAIS, MRS E. M.   Head Teacher, The Kevill–Davies School,
Little Plumstead Hospital, Norwich NOR 52Z, Norfolk
Telephone: Norwich 713355   Ext: 294

PARTICIPANTS

BIRCHALL, MISS E. M.   Area Director of Social Work, 2A Sheep
Street, Bicester, Oxfordshire
Telephone: Bicester 42211

COOMBES, F.   Nursing Officer, (In Charge of Community Services)
Royal Earlswood Hospital, Redhill, Surrey, RH1 6JL
Telephone: Redhill 63591

CROZIER, MRS M.   Senior Advisory and Counselling Officer,
NSMHC, Pembridge Hall, 17 Pembridge Square, London W2 4EP
Telephone: 01-229 8941

DALE, MISS FRANCES   Administrative Secretary, National
Federation of Gateway Clubs, NSMHC, Pembridge Hall, 17
Pembridge Square, London W2 4EP
Telephone: 01-229 8941

DICKS, MISS J.   Social Worker, East Sussex Social Services, Social
Services Area Office, Denmark Villas, Hove, Sussex
Telephone: Brighton 721821

FRIEND, MRS M.   Social Worker, Cambridgeshire and Isle of Ely
Social Services, County Hall, Hobson Street, Cambridge
Telephone: Cambridge 65836   Ext: 34

JONES, MRS S.   Ward Sister, Leavesden Hospital, Abbots Langley,
Watford, Hertfordshire
Telephone: Garston 72222

KEEPING, J.   Senior Social Worker, Tatchbury Mount Hospital,
Calmore, Southampton
Telephone: Ower 441

LAING, W.   Assistant Chief Male Nurse, St Ebba's Hospital,
Epsom, Surrey
Telephone: Epsom 22212

MEADOWS, MRS J.   Matron, Grenfell Hostel (for the Mentally
Handicapped) Ray Park Road, Maidenhead, Berkshire
Telephone: Maidenhead 35456

MEADOWS, T. W.   Superintendent, Grenfell Hostel (for the Mentally Handicapped) Ray Park Road, Maidenhead, Berkshire
Telephone: Maidenhead 35456

SALT, CONRAD   Publicity Assistant, NSMHC, Pembridge Hall, 17
Pembridge Square, London W2 4EP
Telephone: 01-229 8941

REFERENCES

	page	lines
MARAIS, E. 'Cast adrift' (9th August 1973) New Society.	83	2
NATIONAL COUNCIL OF SOCIAL SERVICE: 'The voluntary worker in the social services' (1969) The Aves Report: Report of a Committee jointly set up by the National Council for Social Service and the National Institute of Social Work Training. The Bedford Square Press and George Allen and Unwin.	92	24
McCULLOCH, T. L. 'Reformation of the problem of mental deficiency' (1947) American Journal of Mental Deficiency.	92	36

EMPLOYMENT FOR THE MENTALLY HANDICAPPED

Session Editor: A J Curtis

Senior Executive Officer for Resettlement (Development), Rehabilitation and Resettlement Branch, Employment Service Agency

Department of Employment (DE)

Prior to the Information Exchange Session Mr A. J. Curtis tabled documents which are summarised:

A background briefing on services for disabled workers which describes legislative provision, the Register, the Quota System, designated occupations, and the functions of the disablement advisory committees. Describes industrial rehabilitation units, vocational training and sheltered employment provisions; also the Youth Employment Service, (now the Careers Service), and training for handicapped young people.

A brief guide on mental handicap for disablement resettlement officers which explains the difference between mental handicap and mental illness, summarises the causes of mental handicap, deals with the transition from school to work and provides notes on adult training centres. Guidance is also given on how to advise prospective employers of mentally handicapped people.

A D. of E. discussion paper dealing with resettlement policy and services for disabled people which reviews the disabled population, outlines present policy, and summarises possible changes. Of particular importance (page 110), is the Table giving the estimated annual number of boys and girls aged 16 and 17 leaving special schools in England and Wales analysed by handicap category. The figure for the mentally handicapped, which excludes all ESN (severe), who were not transferred to the educational services at the dates given, and all ESN in special classes in ordinary schools, is 5,366 in a total of 7,447 handicapped school-leavers. This figure

99

confirms that there are more mentally handicapped school-leavers than in the ten other categories shown on the table added together:— that is – approximately 72% of all leavers shown on the table are mentally handicapped. With regard to mentally handicapped adults the Discussion Paper points out that 'Mentally handicapped people represent a problem which is attracting increasing attention particularly as many now survive to be much older and particularly also because the policy of providing community supporting services means that fewer mentally handicapped people will be living in institutions'. The Discussion Document refers to a recent White Paper proposed expenditure of some £100 million. This, from 1971 to 1975, is to be spent on improvements in the hospital and local authority services for the mentally handicapped. It will include further substantial expenditure on local authority adult training centres. These provided 10,000 places in 1960 and 26,400 places in 1970. Of the mentally handicapped in these adult centres only a quarter are more than thirty years old and, when the quality of assessment in these centres improves, it is anticipated that an increasing proportion will be found capable of entering the employment field.

A consultative document reviews the present operation of the Quota Scheme, its weaknesses and its strengths. It considers the abolition of the Quota Scheme (the abolition of compulsion upon employers to take disabled workers) and the possible dangers of this action. It reviews the situation in other countries, and notes that, for example, in Canada, Australia, New Zealand, the United States and Sweden there are no employment schemes based on statutory requirements for employers to engage a quota of disabled people. The Department wished to obtain the views of the National Advisory Council and all other interested organisations, and individuals, upon this Consultative Document. The present Information Exchange Session may raise aspects of this problem for discussion. None of the participants, however, referred to use having been made of the present Quota Scheme in assisting in the placement of mentally handicapped persons in employment.

A folder listing a range of illustrated publications, some designed to promote the interest of employers in disabled workers, some designed to encourage and guide disabled persons in need of training and placement. A leaflet on the mentally handicapped, designed to promote the interest of employers, was considered some time ago by the Department, and co-operation with the preparation of this was given by the NSMHC. Publication has been delayed, however, due to lack of available funds for the printing.

The Disablement Resettlement Service. Referring to the information source provided above (Services for Disabled Workers) following the Department's reorganisation of placing services for disabled workers nearly everywhere in Britain, fully-trained disablement resettlement officers are engaged exclusively in resettlement duties. At February 1972 460 DRO's were employed on full-time resettlement, with a further 77 on part-time duties.

The Session Editor explained that he was associated with a Departmental working party, which, together with the National Advisory Council on the Employment of the Disabled, was preparing a plan to further improve the DRO Service. Consideration was being given to improved methods of recruitment, to an extended training programme and to the possibility of the introduction of a limited career structure within the service. There were a number of other projects which had particular relevance to mental handicap. Firstly, there was the provision, as a small number of industrial rehabilitation units, of young peoples' work preparation courses, where school leavers spent one term half time in further education and half time in the unit workshops. A relatively new idea, they had been remarkably successful and almost all entrants had been mentally handicapped young people. Secondly, there was at the North Nottinghamshire College of Further Education, Worksop, a unique (at this stage) provision for handicapped school leavers in a work preparation scheme for up to 200 entrants. The students are integrated as far as possible with the other college students but form a distinctive unit under their own senior instructor for such special provision as they each require. A large proportion of the present 80 students are ex ESN school-leavers. The course provides a mix of further education, social training and work preparation. Also described was sheltered employment provision for people with mental handicap and epilepsy in special 'parks' schemes in a small number of local authorities. Financially supported by DE these local authorities had devised schemes where severely handicapped people could work in the municipal parks and gardens under special supervision. Leeds had been the first (in 1960) followed by Sheffield, Bradford, Rochdale and more recently Leicester, Nottingham and the London Borough of Havering.

Extended assessment with work preparation. Participants expressed particular interest in the Industrial Rehabilitation Unit (IRU) young peoples' work preparation courses. The Session Editor submitted the following notes:

These courses are intended primarily to assist school-leavers to settle into permanent employment by introducing them gradually to the conditions they will meet. Young people accepted for these courses are likely to be those who will be ready for work after one term of preparation, and who cannot be catered for by short-term assessment in an IRU. This means, unless circumstances are exceptional, that most entrants will be in the higher ESN range. Entrants must have reached school-leaving age conditions before beginning a course. The LEA provides a full-time teacher to work in the IRU and the Department of Employment provides classroom facilities alongside the workshop facilities. A specially selected Departmental Instructor controls the course but when the young people have made sufficient progress in their special section they are transferred to work in other sections of the Unit where they work alongside adults to widen their experience and improve their confidence. Rehabilitation allowances and travelling expenses are met by the Department. Midday meals and protective clothing are provided free of charge.

Courses exist at present in the following IRU's: Bellshill, Billingham, Coventry, Glasgow, Hull, Killingworth, Leeds, Long Eaton, Manchester, Port Talbot, Sheffield.

Matters arising from discussion. In presenting these information sources, brief reference was made to the following points:

Assessment. The positive need for 'in depth' assessment for each mentally handicapped person coming into the employment field; this well before the time of placement.

Work preparation. The need for work preparation prior to employment: over period of months, rather than weeks.

Placement. The need for a comprehensive placement service, in contrast to that which is not uniformly good.

Also, measures to avoid duplication of services. Only rarely, with regard to the mentally handicapped, did the DE services operate smoothly. This left initiative in the hands of others; in particular, nonstatutory organisations.

For example, the London Borough of Croydon, an outstanding model of achievement in respect of the training and employment of the mentally handicapped, had appointed its own Employment Placement Officer. The Session Editor undertook to look at the reasons for this situation.

Remploy Limited. Remploy is a non-profit making concern subject to the direction of the DE and the Treasury. In February 1972 there were 90 factories in Great Britain giving employment to over 7,500 severely disabled people. Currently about 20% of the work force are mentally ill. About 10% are mentally handicapped, although the majority of these are in the mildly handicapped category. The criteria for admission to sheltered employment with Remploy is more flexible than is generally thought. For example, the determination to do good work and to work hard may be more important than a person's actual ability, to carry out certain operations. Many of the production processes are designed to accommodate the more grevious handicaps providing that social competence and work attitude is sound. The old concept of 2/3 of normal piecework may no longer apply. Assessment of applicants should have reference to the work that they will actually need to do: general work assessment is of little value. It was pointed out that Industrial Rehabilitaion Units (there are 25 under the DE and 14,000 pass through each year) cannot be used to prepare persons for sheltered employment, only for open employment. It would be valuable if the DE could consider this point.

The Employment Medical Advisory Service (EMAS). This is a service established by the DE in February 1973 under the Employment Medical Advisory Service Act 1972. EMAS is concerned with the study of the medical requirements for work, especially in relation to disabled persons, and with giving advice to general practitioners, and – in co-operation with Careers Officers and Schools Medical Officers (now transferred to restructured National Health Service; see NHS below). EMAS will also give advice to the DE placing, training and resettlement service, and to employers on any medical problems in connection with the employment of disabled persons. The Service has a staff of 100 doctors, full or part-time. The new system is designed to concentrate medical advice on those young people who need it in relation to their employment. It covers all kinds of work, not only employment under the Factories Act, and relies on close co-operation between the Schools Health Service, the Careers Service, General Practitioners and the Medical Advisory Service. Attention was also drawn to the information provided by the Department of Education and Science which outlines how the new service (EMAS) ties in for severely handicapped pupils, and particularly those likely to require special help.

The Youth Employment Service. Advice on employment and placement, usually initiated two years before school-leaving, is available to ESN Special School pupils up to 18 years of age, or beyond if the young person remains at school. The possibility of the Youth Employment Service being merged with the DE has not materialised, so that following re-organisation in April 1974 guidance will be provided everywhere by local education authorities. However, following the first placement of a school-leaver, it will be possible in future for the individual school-leaver to choose whether to use the Youth Service or the Department of Employment for further guidance on training and employment.

For the average school-leaver it was thought this opportunity for choice might be of value, but for the handicapped leaver, who may not be able to exercise choice, and may indeed require positive follow-up, it was thought that the change would only confuse more the already unsatisfactory separation of the three services which are each concerned with making their contribution to placement (i.e. the School: the Youth Service: the DE, Special Services Branch).

Need for continuity in records. In view of the separation of these (and other services) and the possible failure of really effective co-ordination, continuity of records held by the appropriate Social Services Department in the area of residence, is essential. A social worker said her files carried, in addition to educational, medical and social records, the records of assessments and contributions made by other organisations.

The Department of Health and Social Security

Queen Alexandria Hospital: Portsmouth. A useful model, which might prove of value for future development, was the attachment of a District Resettlement Officer (DRO), by arrangement with the Department of Employment, to this hospital. It was, however, pointed out that the main concern at the Queen Alexandria was the rehabilitation and work placement of the physically handicapped and not the mentally handicapped.

Hospitals for the mentally handicapped: Bromham Hospital, Bedford. A good relationship existed with the responsible DRO. But the problem was not only securing employment for trained patients, but also the necessary residential facilities. There was only one adult hostel for the mentally handicapped in Bedfordshire. Some effort had been made by the hospital to exchange competent residents (from the hospital) for those residing in the community who were more grievously handicapped and in need of special care, but as these special care cases were frequently still associated with their families, parents actively resisted this suggestion. This was unfortunate as it would clearly be to the advantage of those more able patients still in hospital, who could settle in open employment, if only residential facilities in the community were available to them.

St Ebba's Hospital, Epsom. This position was even more acute in hospitals placed in areas where neither accommodation nor employment was available for the able patients; 30 out of 180 patients were ready for community life in a hostel and possible employment, but sites for hostel development could not be found in the stockbroker belt, and employment in the area was also not available, due to the absence of industry.

Discussion. The Session Editor mentioned the idea of village communities, which could be sited in areas where both accommodation and work might be available, and where land could be purchased at reasonable prices. Several participants opposed village communities on the grounds that they were unnatural and unfair to the mentally handicapped. It was suggested that the mentally handicapped should always have the opportunity to participate, to whatever degree they may be capable, in the life of the normal community. The siting of work and residential facilities in close proximity was also thought to be a bad thing. Work place and residence should be quite separate.

A Token Reward System operating in St Ebba's Hospital was described and attention drawn to certain unsatisfactory aspects of this system.

Details were also given (Farleigh Hospital, Bristol) of the uses of 'reward money' and its relation to personal allowances for those placed in employment outside the hospital. Farleigh Hospital is eight miles from Bristol and, given open employment, the cost of board and lodgings is so high that the patient could be better off unemployed on a social security allowance. This was part of a wider problem which reflected the low wages paid for some jobs. Development of Negative Income Tax, or Tax Credits might help to overcome this problem. The 'token reward system' and all other associated financial schemes, available to patients in hospitals, are described fully in the NAMH paper: Rehabilitation for Employment.

It was noted that with the re-organisation of the National Health Service, although general practitioners, schools medical officers, and community physicians, will all come under the new organisation, the records required for assessment, and for placement in training and employment, will still be available. The organisation of social security benefits, national insurance and the attendance allowance will remain under existing departments. No indication was given by participants as to what information links – if any – exist between these services, and social service departments.

Social service departments
Discussion. It was suggested that a directory, similar to that provided by the NSMHC listing residential accommodation for the mentally handicapped could be valuable, as an information source, in listing the training and work-preparation courses at present available in the United Kingdom; these from both statutory and non-statutory organisations. When the services available for the placement of the mentally handicapped broke down, as they frequently did, parents suffered severe anxiety, with a child at home, having left school, but without prospects or a future.

In many cases the job problem had not been properly thought out by parents and in many cases insufficient information had reached them in the years before school-leaving from teachers in the school responsible for careers guidance, or from the other services concerned. Reference at this point was made to information recently made available. Much could be done by social workers to ensure that these gaps were covered by advice and made easier by early, rather than late, references to the proper agencies. Under the 1944 Education Act, local education authorities had a duty to identify, at age two years, those children who would be in need of special education, when at an age to receive it. Records could be made available to local authority social workers, who could then ensure that 'gaps' could be watched, and advisory action taken. The Elfred Thomas Report in fact recommended (page 168) that responsibility for seeing that the necessary services are provided and co-ordinated should rest with the local authority.

For this kind of co-ordination effective records are required. The ethical and legal aspects of confidentiality of personal records was currently a matter of much professional concern. The Youth Employment Service (now Careers Service) destroy all records of clients reaching 21 years of age. The problem was to ensure that the information given to helping agencies was sufficient for proper assessment and placement whilst information on (say) delinquency or a poor prognosis was restricted to a proper use. There was not likely to be a clear-cut solution to this problem. It was important to ensure that the permission of parent or guardian was obtained before full records were sought or given. It would be unfortunate if, in an excess of concern for confidentiality, personal records, which might lead to the effective progress of a client through the various agencies, were either not kept, or not made available at the right time. This would apply even where information gives indications contrary to a client's placement in employment. It was recognised that further information sources were needed on this topic.

With regard to the suggestion that a directory of training and work preparation courses should be considered, the following organisations were proposed for inclusion:

Turners Court, Oxford. Vocational training community for 120 boys age 15/18. Established 60 years. 'Many boys are casualties of the education system.'

Derwen Training College and Workshops, Oswestry. Residential training of physically or mentally disabled school-leavers (boys and girls) who are capable of some kind of work: sheltered workshop for those who cannot be employed in open industry.

The Queen Elizabeth's Foundation for the Disabled, Leatherhead, Surrey. A report by this Foundation refers to a variety of provisions for school-leavers who are disabled, but does not indicate the degree of mental handicap acceptable. Organisations mentioned include the Queen Elizabeth Training College: Dorincourt Sheltered Workshop; St Loye's College, Exeter (25 boys, 25 girls); Red Cross Houses – Largs and Inverness: there will also be those where mental handicap may be a secondary disability, as the Chalfont Centre for Epilepsy, etc. A finding in this report is that: 'The manner in which the handicapped school-leaver is referred, and the process by which he or she arrives at the correct level of employment, be it in open industry, or sheltered employment, or even in residential welfare workshops, is haphazard and inconsistent.'

Local Authority Adult Training Centres — Under Directors of Social Service

There was a considerable divergence in the information provided concerning adult training centres where it was recognised that more than 95% of the ESN (Severe) who remain in the community over school-leaving age, would be likely to find themselves placed, as things stand at present, for the rest of their lives. To this number must also be added the failed ESN school-leavers (about 10% of all ESN school-leavers) who have been found by their authorities as unsuitable for either open employment or sheltered work. 'Abandon hope, all ye who enter here' was the attitude of a number of participants. A Careers Officer informed the Session that he used every possible effort to keep the younger mentally handicapped outside of adult training centres. The mixture of old and young, of degrees of disability, and of kinds of personality difficulty can often lead to a depressing and defeatist labelling of a whole group as 'the mentally handicapped'. Prospects for the individual human being can be lost under these circumstances. Particular concern was expressed at the increase in the rate of overcrowding in adult centres, the lengthening waiting list, and the general lack of hope for any improvement in a worsening situation. The problem was not helped by the presence of parents who were naturally anxious.

In complete contrast to this kind of information was the description given of the Work Preparation for Open Employment Scheme at the Edmonton Adult Training Centre, (London Borough of Enfield). This development, and the remarkable progress made over the years was particularly associated with the work of Dr Guy Wigley, then Medical Officer of Health, Middlesex County Council. In Edmonton the Adult Training Centre, which has a usual daily attendance of 130 trainees is closely associated with a large engineering factory in the Borough. One of the departments in this factory is set aside for ongoing work preparation courses for severely subnormal trainees in a realistic factory working situation; the Instructor-in-charge of this Work Preparation Department is a member of the Training Centre Staff, seconded to this duty on a full-time basis. The work preparation group comprise fifteen trainees who have first to complete a satisfactory course of social and work training within the main Training Centre. On completion of their work preparation – during which they remain the responsibility of the Training Centre and are in receipt of social security allowances, they can – if they are successful – then pass through to the production departments of the factory and take up normal paid employment; this in a work situation which is not only familiar to them, but where they are already accepted by their working colleagues.

Also described were go-ahead schemes for Group Work Projects; schemes for the encouragement of small groups, near to employment levels, in pre-work group activities, and examples of effective co-operation with the Youth Employment Service (now Careers Service): also effective co-operation between the Adult Centre and College of Further Education (one day a week for two years to overcome emotional and social problems). Finally, information was provided on the provisions made by the London Borough of Croydon. Here a go-ahead local authority had proved that effective provision for adult training, assessment and employment could be made.

The London Borough of Croydon. Outline of provisions:—

Waylands Centre. This is one of the three kinds of Unit provided. With a population of approximately 300,000 a greater variety of the requisite specialised units to deal with all aspects of assessment, work and suitable training can be provided. It should be noted however, that even with this considerable size of catchment area, to justify this kind of sophistication in the services, the mentally retarded, the physically handicapped and the mentally ill are mixed, (in the sheltered work situation, but not in training).

At this Centre, initial assessment, training and further education is provided with particular emphasis on social education. Coaches are provided to take the trainees to and from the Centre, although those capable of making their own way are encouraged to do so. The Waylands Centre cost nearly £250,000 to build and accommodate 120 mentally handicapped and 80 physically handicapped adults.

Waylands provides occupation for some of the most severely retarded of the mentally handicapped. The Centre's classes are graded according to ability, but no-one is excluded because their handicap is too profound. Waylands has its own small laundry which provides a service for the old people's homes in the district.

Cherry Orchard. Trainees graduating from Waylands Centre are moved to an intermediate training centre – Cherry Orchard, where more advanced industrial training is undertaken. Trainees may advance yet again, if they profit from this intermediate training, to the Crosfield Industrial Training Unit. Here employment is provided, and also special industrial rehabilitation to assist the handicapped to obtain open employment.

Crosfield Industrial Unit. The Crosfield Unit has its own Industrial Welfare Officer who is responsible for the follow-up of trainees who have found employment in open industry. A Placing Officer is also provided with particular responsibility for the finding of suitable jobs. The Unit accommodates 136 handicapped persons, of whom 48 are mentally handicapped, 65 are mentally ill and 23 are physically handicapped. In the Crosfield Industrial Unit the Trade Union Shop Steward is a physically handicapped man suffering from quadriplegia and all the handicapped are given the opportunity of joining a trade union. In cases where persons are incapable of making this judgement, parents are asked to make a decision on their behalf.

Discussion. The Session Editor was asked if the DE have in fact issued guidance to local authorities on the need to split up their provisions, as done by Croydon, into the appropriate areas of occupation, training, work readiness, assessment and sheltered workshop facilities. The Session Editor said that details of the financial support available to local social service departments were already in the hands of local authorities and the Department was always prepared to listen to proposals that local authorities wish to put forward.

In this connection a special issue of Parent's Voice, the Journal of the NSMHC, was tabled, devoted to the training and employment of the mentally handicapped. In it an article clearly defines the areas of special need of Groups A, B and C, as follows:—

Group A. School-leavers: age 16–18.

Group B. Adults who are so handicapped that, at present, there is no hope that they could work, even in sheltered conditions.

Group C. Those for which sheltered work conditions are required.

The article then deals specifically with the education and training of Group A, with specific reference to the findings of the Slough Project.

Department of Education and Science

Special schools for the ESN and ESN (Severe). In order to limit the present Information Exchange to reasonable numbers, representatives from special schools and the education services had not been invited to the current Information Exchange Session. It had been noted, however, by contributors from the Youth Employment Service (now Careers Service), and others, that there was under development in education authorities a variety of employment readiness projects in special schools. In particular an outstanding Portsmouth development which, although launched by a grant from non-statutory sources (The Sembal Trust) had now been taken over by the local education authority. Provision is made for ESN school-leavers, who are unready for employment at school-leaving age (16 years) to take up vocational and social training under simulated industrial conditions. Direct links are kept with the Youth Employment Service (now Careers Service) and the aim is to keep boys and girls until 17 years of age (exceptionally for a longer period) until they can be placed in jobs which they will be likely to hold. The Industrial Training Unit (at Cliffdale School) accommodates 24 pupils and eight had been satisfactorily placed in employment at the end of term. The project is under the direction of Mr Jerrold. Information was requested concerning those children with emotional problems or other multiple handicaps who may not be suitable for open employment at the completion of the course. It was explained that the Industrial Training Experiment was not for problem children: they have to be able to hold their place and benefit from the instruction given. Those who do not secure open employment at 17 years pass on to the Adult Training Centre provided by the Local Authority Social Service Department. The question was raised as to what was the proper provision for young persons who failed to reach 'employable level' and were also unsuited to sheltered work. It was thought that research might be needed in this area to establish the most effective kind of programme for this non-employable non-work group.

Colleges of Further Education. It was suggested that a variety of Colleges of Further Education throughout the country were now developing remedial courses of further education for mentally handicapped school-leavers in the high-achievement range. An example was given of the Hammersmith College of Further Education. It was suggested that facilities such as this, where they existed, might also be listed in a guide for social workers, careers officers and other concerned persons. This information could be included in the kind of directory already proposed. The nine or ten Industrial Rehabilitation Units mentioned by the Session

Editor, which are run almost exclusively for mentally handicapped young people, might also be listed in such a document.

National Association for Mental Health

A heavy demand was reported, mainly from social workers, for more training schemes – day and residential – for the lower grade ESN. There was a substantial demand for these courses which is not being met. There was also need for diversification in training programmes. Why is so much of it industrial training? What about training for residential and domestic services? More effective and more easily available work assessment courses were also required, and one central department, or at least one record file, would be of value. Reference was made to two recent information documents published by the NAMH.

One provides, in brief form, a complete introduction to all the services and provisions, together with the categories of financial arrangements, available to all classes of the disabled. The second presents NAMH policy with regard to the (then) current Government proposals for changes in the services for the disabled. Although there was frequent reference to the complexity of present services, the main recommendation of the above Report – 'that there should be a new Disablement Service – under a responsible Minister' – was, at no time, given support by the participants. Perhaps the suggestion, made from several sources, that there should (instead) be an effective system of records, which might achieve the same objective of co-ordination, indicated the preference of participants.

The tendency to confuse the needs of the mentally ill, which are highly specialised, with those of the mentally handicapped, which call for a widely different specialised approach, in all provisions (except perhaps in sheltered workshops) is unsatisfactory, and may lead to confused thinking in the future development of more effective services for the mentally handicapped.

National Elfrida Rathbone Society

The Wapping Employment Readiness Project designed for educationally handicapped school-leavers was described. The Project proved to be a valuable demonstration of what can be done, in any city or town, and the novel methods that can be tried, to introduce young people to the benefits of participation, and of making their contribution to society. The Project covered a period of fifteen days; further projects will cover a period of five weeks.

National Society for Mentally Handicapped Children

NSMHC training establishments. The Lufton Manor Rural Training Unit was briefly described. The Unit runs a two-year course for young men and young women from high range ESN to middle range ESN (severe). The course is residential and leisure development, social training and adjustment, are all fully integrated with the vocational training provided. The placement rate of graduates is at present running at 60%. The special issue of 'Parent's Voice' (tabled – see page 117) describes fully, in an article written by the Director, the background to this Project. The same journal also includes information on other NSMHC Projects, including the Advanced Social Training Unit at Dilston Hall and the Preparation for Work Courses at Pengwern Hall. The same issue carries an article by the NSMHC's Director of Education and Training looking back at the NSMHC's Slough Experiment.

South Wales. Information was given of a novel scheme launched by the South Wales and Monmouthshire Region of the NSMHC. The scheme will be based on the principle that the training for employment required by the mentally handicapped could best be given by sympathetic employers, who would be paid for their training services. The advantage of the scheme would be that, whilst it would not cost more than training the mentally handicapped in training centres, it would ensure that they are trained in the actual practical work situation to which they will have to adjust, if they are to secure full-time open employment. The Region launched an Appeal to raise money for a project which was abandoned. The Appeal raised £25,000 which, when invested, will yield sufficient revenue to maintain eighteen young men and young women in work training placements with actual employers; six trainees will come from hospitals; six from training centres and six from the lower group of ESN school-leavers. All entrants will be given a 3 month course of intensive social training and work assessment before they are introduced to their in-situ employment training situations. The period of training will be 12 weeks and the Foreman-in-charge of the trainee's development will also receive a payment. The age range of entrants will be 16 to 25 years and the payment will be £50 to the responsible foreman and £212 to the employers.

Discussion. It was suggested, in providing advice and information to parents of mentally handicapped children, that they should be fully prepared for dealing with the problems of employment before these problems arise. It is essential, if parents are to adopt the right attitude to the proper placement of their child, that they should be realistic and well-informed. Examples were given of young people leaving school who were seriously misplaced for a variety of reasons. Young people had been placed in office work when they really needed work in the open air: particularly regretted was the placement of young people in positions which caused them distress, simply because of the unrealistic expectations of others. It should be accepted, by all who work with the mentally handicapped, that effective assessment and effective parent counselling, can be just as valuable in establishing that employment is not possible, as it can be in establishing that employment is possible. Consideration was given to a design and marketing organisation that would permit adult training centres (and Sheltered Workshops) to design and market viable products, as an alternative to the more usual kinds of contract work that is undertaken by most Adult Centres at present.

The Spastics Society

The Placement Services and the assessment and training facilities provided by the Spastics Society were described. There are four placement officers in the United Kingdom; they co-operate, as specialists, wherever possible, with the DRO and with Careers Officers. Not only the school-leavers require adequate assessment, training and placement. People who already have employment also like to change their job from time to time.

The Session Editor writes:

The exchange of information on employment seemed to me to be a highly successful occasion and one with which I was delighted to be associated.

If anyone would like to have further information about the many and various changes going on in the Department of Employment or about the consideration currently being given to particular areas of resettlement policy, I should be pleased if they would contact me at the Department's Headquarters.

During 1974, the DRO Service, integrated with the modernised employment service as part of the Employment Service Agency will be separating from the Department and will be part of the Manpower Services Commission. We are looking forward to being able to give a new improved service to all disabled people and those who are mentally handicapped will be no exception.

I have already discussed with the Secretary to the Information Exchange Session my wish to look again at the possibility of producing, with the help of NSMHC, a leaflet which would be issued to employers and potential employers of mentally handicapped people giving guidance about their special needs and the nature of any special support or supervision they might desirably wish to introduce.

Thank you for your support. I did not know quite what was expected of a session editor but whether or not I fulfilled the intended role adequately the friendly co-operation of all participants certainly made the going easy.

John Curtis

Individual contributions are identified by page and line number on the List of Participants. References are identified by page and line, in the same way.

Participants Lists give the name, address, telephone number and post held at the time the contribution was made.

LIST OF PARTICIPANTS

page *lines*

SESSION EDITOR:

CURTIS, A. J. Senior Executive Officer for Resettlement
(Development), Rehabilitation and Resettlement Branch,
Employment Service Agency

PARTICIPANTS

CARTER, DAVID Director, Lufton Manor Rural Training
Unit, Lufton, Yeovil, Somerset
Telephone: 09-35 3124

106   24–25
112   1– 8

McCONNELL, J. Assistant Chief Male Nurse, Farleigh Hospital,
Flax Bourton, Bristol BS19 3QZ
Telephone: 027-583 2028

105   13–20

DOIDGE, W. L. Regional Officer, NSMHC, South Wales &
Monmouthshire, 31, The Parade, Cardiff CF2 3AD
Telephone 02-22 20668

112   14–34

EVANS, MISS A. London Development Officer, Elfrida Rathbone
Society, 17, Victoria Park Square, London E2
Telephone: 01-837 9842

111   30–36

FARROW, MISS H. Manager, Waylands Training Centre, Purley
Way, Croydon, Surrey
Telephone: 01-681 2655

FLINT, MRS D. Regional Officer, NSMHC, Metropolitan Region,
Coventry House, 5/6 Coventry Street, London W1
Telephone: 437 4538/9 or 734 7417/8

112–113   35– 7

FORT, MISS D. Placement Officer, Spastics Society, 16 Fitzroy
Square, London W1P 5HQ
Telephone: 01-387 9571

113   12–18

HAMBRIDGE, F. Manager, Chelmsford Adult Training Centre,
Ravensbourne Drive, Chelmsford, Essex
Telephone: 0245 57155

HATTERSLEY-SMITH, N. Deputy Senior Careers Officer, Special
Careers Service, Youth Employment Services, 45, Sidmouth
Street, London WC1
Telephone: 01-837 9842

103   9–13
103–104   32– 7
106   16–23

HEPPER, MRS A. Social Worker, Advisory Casework Service,
National Association for Mental Health, 39 Queen Anne Street,
London W1M oAV
Telephone: 01-935 1272

111   3–11

HOLMES, P. J. Specialist Senior Careers Officer, London Borough
of Hillingdon, Belmont House, High Street, 38 Market Square,
Uxbridge
Telephone: Uxbridge 38232

107   21–28

HUNT, MISS H. Assistant Regional Officer, NSMHC, Metropolitan
Region, Coventry House, 5/6 Coventry Street, London W1
Telephone: 437 4538/9 or 734 7417/8

116

REFERENCES

	page	lines
DEPARTMENT OF EMPLOYMENT: 'Services for disabled workers' (1972) Background briefing No. 5.	99	3
DEPARTMENT OF EMPLOYMENT: 'Mental handicap' (1972) Disablement Resettlement Officers guide No. 5.	99	10
DEPARTMENT OF EMPLOYMENT: 'Resettlement policy and services for disabled people' (1972).	99	16
DEPARTMENT OF HEALTH AND SOCIAL SECURITY: 'Better services for the mentally handicapped' (1971) Cmnd 4683 HMSO.	100	11
DEPARTMENT OF EMPLOYMENT: Folder of publications and leaflets related to disablement (1973).	100	36
DEPARTMENT OF EMPLOYMENT: 'The quota scheme for disabled people' (1973) Consultative document.	100	21
DEPARTMENT OF EMPLOYMENT: 'Employment medical advisory service' (1972) Guide to service.	103	29
DEPARTMENT OF EDUCATION AND SCIENCE: Circular M027/49/01D (March 1973) Outlines EMAS services in relation to severely handicapped school-leavers.	103	32
SHENNAN, V. (Ed) 'Directory of residential accommodation for the mentally handicapped in England, Wales and Northern Ireland' (1976) NSMHC.	105	35
TUCKEY, L., PARFITT, J. and TUCKEY, B. 'Handicapped school-leavers: their further education, training and employment' (1973) A National Children's Bureau Report published by the National Federation for Educational Research.	106	5
BRITISH COUNCIL FOR THE REHABILITATION OF THE DISABLED: 'The handicapped school-leaver' (1964) (The Elfred Thomas Report).	106	15
ANON: 'Turner's Court Oxford' (January 30 1970) British Hospital Journal and Social Service Review.	106	35
THE QUEEN ELIZABETH FOUNDATION FOR THE DISABLED: 'Handicapped school-leavers: report of an enquiry' (1972).	107	3
TUDOR-DAVIES, E. R. (Ed) 'Innovations in England and Wales' (1973) Lecture notes with colour slides NSMHC.	108	24
GUNZBURG, H. C. 'Education for work and life' (September 1973) 'Parent's Voice': The Journal of the NSMHC.	109	40
BARANYAY, E. P. 'The mentally handicapped adolescent' (1971) Pergamon Press.	109	40
MIND: 'Rehabilitation for employment and sheltered work for the mentally, physically and socially disabled: a summary and definition of terms' (March 1973)	111	11
MIND: 'Jobs—but not for the disabled' (October 1972) Mind Report No. 8.	111	11
THE NATIONAL ELFRIDA RATHBONE ASSOCIATION: 'Annual report' (1972/73)	111	31
GRAY, FRANKLIN, G. 'Advanced social training unit at Dilston Hall' (September 1973) 'Parent's Voice': The Journal of the NSMHC.	112	13
WEINBERG, M. 'Preparation for work courses at Pengwern Hall' (September 1973) 'Parent's Voice': The Journal of the NSMHC.	112	13
CUMMINGS, J. 'Slough in retrospect' (September 1973) 'Parent's Voice': The Journal of the NSMHC.	112	13

THE RESEARCH/PRACTICE GAP

Session Editor: T D Wilson, B Sc (Econ) FL A
Lecturer, University of Sheffield, Postgraduate School of Librarianship and
Information Science

Research past, present and ongoing

Research in the social services

Typical current research projects were described by participants:—

London Borough of Harrow. This Borough is currently researching
into the needs of the mentally handicapped in the Harrow area and
collecting information for future planning. There are 75 patients, now
resident in Harperbury Hospital, who are ultimately the responsibility
of Harrow Social Services, and may some day require community facilities within the Borough.

Berkshire County Council. Berkshire Social Services, with the help
of Reading University are undertaking a project designed to evaluate
provisions for the mentally handicapped in the county. This evaluation
covers not only the statutory services but also facilities run by the private
sector, such as Ravenswood. Information on the basic abilities and behaviour of the mentally handicapped is being collected by means of direct
observation and questionnaires, which are filled in by those who are
familiar with the mentally handicapped persons concerned. In the
allotted three years, the relative effects of the environment on the mentally handicapped will be observed and an attempt will be made to
develop a scale for the measurement of social competence. To maintain
contact with technical expertise the Research Officer is attached to the
Operational Research Unit at Reading University. This Unit is sponsored
directly by the Department of Health and Social Security.

London Borough of Greenwich. A research project, run along the
same lines as the King's Fund Centre's Project, examines the services
provided for the mentally handicapped, inside and outside hospitals.
The aim of this project is to evaluate the existing level of services and

119

secondly to predict future needs and demands. The main purpose of the original King's Fund research project was to look into the co-ordination of services for the mentally handicapped and the presence or absence of such co-ordination, with suggestions/recommendations for improvement. It attempted to give a detailed description of services for the mentally handicapped in seven local authorities, and to develop methods for improving those services through the active involvement of those who provide them.

Research in the health services

Research has been in progress for several years and continues to look into a complexity of factors concerning Wessex's health care provisions. The research is mainly concerned with the evaluation and feasibility of various types of residential care. Methods of assessing the progress of the severely and profoundly subnormal have been developed and question-naires made up with the help of parents, teachers and others. Interviews are lengthy but concerned with reliability and validity. Research is also being done into the problems of parents and families with a mentally handicapped member, both those at home and in residential care. Leng-thy interviews, sometimes taking between 1 and 4 hours, are conducted to gain information on experiences at crucial times in the lives of those concerned with the mentally handicapped. The first admission of a re-tarded child into residential care may be a crucial time.

Independent research

The Institute for Research into Mental and Multiple Handicap. The Institute has recently appointed a research team. It is looking into residential care for mentally handicapped adults.

The Office of Health Economics. OHE was founded in 1962 by the Association of the British Pharmaceutical Industry. Its terms of reference are to undertake research on the economic aspects of medical care; to investigate other health and social problems; to collect data from other countries and to publish results, data and conclusions relevant to the above. One of these research projects was on mental handicap and the results, data and conclusions were published.

The Institute for Consumer Ergonomics. This is a research orga-nisation within Loughborough University. It was established in November 1970 with the objectives of carrying out ergonomic evaluations and design studies on consumer goods, buildings and their fitting and services used by the public. The ultimate aim is to improve standards in these areas for the benefit of the public generally, including children, the elderly and the disabled. The research undertaken by the Institute is carried out on a contract basis; the majority of contracts are from government departments but charities and other organisations also support a substantial amount of work. Research projects take various forms including needs analyses, surveys, equipment evaluation and design and development studies. The Institute is undertaking a survey of toys and play equipment for severely mentally handicapped children in mental handicap hospitals. The main body of research, into aids and equipment for eating activities of children with multiple handicaps, will commence in April 1975. Research into equipment has drawn the attention of research workers to the wider problems of the need for research into the social systems within which the equipment will be used.

Trends in research

The King's Fund Centre Project. By participation in the construction of the King's Fund Centre's research project, those working in the field with the mentally handicapped were able to determine what questions needed to be answered regarding the co-ordination of services for the retarded. The participants represented seven local authorities and came from many different levels of bureaucracy from junior front-line workers to senior administrators. They belonged to nearly all the professions involved in the care and treatment of the mentally handicapped. Seven different questionnaires were constructed with the help of participants who knew what sort of information ought to be collected. These questionnaires were for parents, teachers, paediatricians, health visitors, mental welfare officers and others. One was also constructed for the records' file! This was done to determine whether the records contained relevant data. This participative method led to the emergence of an awareness of the weaknesses and strengths of different roles in relation to co-ordination. The participants were capable of self-criticism and even before an analysis of the research could be produced action was taking place on the job.

The Office of Health Economics Report. The Office of Health Economics in a recent report states that 'techniques already exist, which if applied on a nationwide scale, would probably cut by more than 50% the annual incidence of severe mental handicap and relieve many other cases'. The motivation behind the Association of the British Pharmaceutical Industry sponsoring the Office of Health Economics is one of maximising sale while minimising risk. It was thought that this type of free enterprise may have certain advantages in the field of mental retardation. Firstly, free enterprise would control research through different management techniques by setting certain targets and limits such as cost and safety. Secondly, it was thought that research findings would be brought to the public more quickly. There were merits of choice in a free market for those concerned with the mentally handicapped. Certain services are obviously best co-ordinated and provided by the Government but others could be provided in a free market where the choice would be made by those requiring the service. Good services would presumably thrive while others, not so popular, would cease to exist; but there should be some check on the quality of services provided in this free market. The suggestion, put forward by the Disablement Income Group and others, is that the Government should raise the amount of discretionary income they give to enable recipients to choose between services being provided through this proposed system of free enterprise.

The Department of Health and Social Security. The kernel of general strategy expressed in the White Paper 'Better Services for the Mentally Handicapped', is a gradual shift in emphasis from a pattern of service which is largely hospital based to much greater emphasis and reliance upon care within the community. This means increased provision of services and capital facilities – homes and training sectors – by local authorities. This policy has important implications for research activity which may be sponsored by the DHSS. Within the last year the DHSS has set up a number of research liaison groups, among them one to deal with mental health including mental handicap research. The Liaison Group includes individuals from outside the DHSS with particular experience in the area of mental handicap and a central component of its activity is to ensure that Departmental research sponsorship is related as effectively as possible to topics relevant to current policy development. It will have direct application to 'service delivery'. The DHSS is at present sponsoring a very wide range of research in the mental handicap field. Particular emphasis is being laid upon evaluation of existing services and upon feasibility studies of service needs and provision for mentally handicapped people and their families. While these are thought to be priority areas for research it does not imply that research in other areas, e.g. aetiology, will be ignored. While the Research Liaison Group will operate to improve the co-ordination of research and policy development the total research programme will continue to be broadly based.

Discussion. In a review of research and practice in the teaching and training of severely mentally handicapped children in hospitals for the subnormal. Peter Cummings, its author, concluded 'Finally the question remains "For whom do the writers write?" The intended readers are clearly indicated or implied in the various texts. Then who actually reads them?

For the moment the answer must be, largely students, research workers and – other writers!' Perhaps the same applied to researchers. It may be that researchers do their research for other research workers. Dr Mia Kellmer Pringle, when talking about the education situation, said she would put a ban on research in this field and start applying the findings that are already known. There is a stock pile of research findings still not applied in special education. Many people regarded research as a 'sacred cow'. Some research may be motivated by social factors or hunches not declared in the research. It may be that findings on similar research are different in the same area. Politically based findings, if incorrect, would soon be pulled to pieces by other researchers. There seemed to be several research projects going on in different parts of the country looking into the same subject. Was there scope for co-ordination of research? Was repetition of certain research projects around the country a bad thing? Different researchers will attack different aspects of the same problem; a useful exercise in itself. Findings in Berkshire may not necessarily be applicable to any other county in the country due to differences of ecological background and so on. There may, however, be some useful 'spin-off'. It was pointed out that there could be a wider sharing of research techniques. For instance, the Berkshire questionnaire was closely based on the Wessex questionnaire. Harrow were using the questionnaire being used in hospitals by Greenwich. This was designed by nurses and doctors, social workers and parents so that those applying the questionnaire were not unduly hampered in their daily rush to get the job done. Questions are simple for day to day answers. Could researchers in the field of mental handicap apply the different techniques used in areas of technology, to their field?

Duplication. Duplication was not a cause for concern. People involved in research are going through learning processes and this, in itself, will cause action through self-education and the education of others at the same time. On the other hand, duplicated research was not cumulative; researchers were not gaining from the previous experience of others. The DHSS were not keen to spend money duplicating research just for the sake of education. Co-ordination with accumulation was more important. It was a pity that research into genetics was no longer a priority, when a breakthrough in reducing the number of mentally handicapped was so near.

Causes of the research/practice gap

The Session Editor opened the Afternoon Session by stating his interest in the transfer of information, whether orally or in writing, to those who will use it. He lectures on a MA Course at Sheffield University which is concerned with information problems in the social sciences and which prepares people for work in a variety of environments, including local authority social services departments.

Discussion. Communicators needed to know more about research. The research message never sees the light of day. Could researchers use journals to get their message over to the public? There were several requests for the 'translation' of research findings into comprehensible and digestable information for the layman who would, ultimately, be implementing findings. Research work, when reported through journals, is in technical language; unfortunately researchers did not see it as part of their job to hand on the information they had found. There were however plenty of people interpreting and translating research for publication in magazines. Nevertheless, not only was there a communication gap between research worker and research worker but also between research worker and practitioner. It was clear from the work in Greenwich that there is evidence to show that approximately one in ten parents in the community have more than one handicapped child in their family. Yet it is also clear that, although this is the case, many parents are not offered family planning facilities. It may be that they do not even receive genetic counselling. Support may be there but the knowledge of general practitioners, social workers and others is not sufficient. How do we get the information to them?

Intentional research/practice gaps? With regard to the suggestion that better communication could overcome apparent research/practice gaps, is it possible that some of these gaps are not due to failure of communication, but are purposeful, and are intended to protect the public? Under 'Foetal Delay' Guardian 20th November, 1974 Robin Laurence suggested there may be some evidence that this situation does exist:—

'Since it became possible to detect both mongolism and spina bifida in a foetus reasonably early in pregnancy, and since the law made it possible to terminate such pregnancies when the risk of an abnormal birth is substantial, mothers have had every opportunity to choose between having a severely handicapped child or not having a child at all. One in three British children born subnormal are mongols, and 2,000 are born with spina bifida every year, yet few women are seeking advice. And what appears to be a curious lack of response from mothers turns out to be simply a lack of publicity about the tests, according to Professor M. A. Ferguson-Smith, of the Medical Genetics Department at Glasgow University, who accused some doctors of actively discouraging their patients from seeking advice. The test, called amniocentesis, involves taking a sample of fluid from the amnion (birth sac) during the sixteenth week of pregnancy. It has been found reliable in detecting both mongolism and spina bifida along with a number of other rarer abnormalities.

In theory, mongolism and spina bifida could be wiped out by screening every woman who becomes pregnant and then aborting the affected foetuses. The frequency of mongolism among the new-born is about one in 600. But such is the importance of maternal age that a woman of 40 stands a one-in-40 chance of having a mongol child. And a mother who already has had a spina bifida child runs a one-in-20 risk of having another. Yet many parents don't know about the tests. Some doctors claim that the test still carries an element of risk. So did the Department of Health in reply to the National Association for Mental Health, which is pressing for a localised pilot screening programme. Yet the specialists say the risks are 'minimal' and a group of leading obstetricians and geneti-cists have already recommended the Department to make provision for a 'comprehensive diagnostic service' to keep pace with an ex-pected increase in demand. The Government insists, however, that it would be 'unwise to encourage widespread expansion' before the Medical Research Council, which is studying the procedures in a number of centres, comes up with its report. But the Department is clearly in two minds about the caution it advocated, since it has made a direct grant of £30,000 to Queen Charlotte's Hospital in West London for a new pre-natal diagnostic clinic which will incorporate the very tests it claims to have doubts about. But there are also doubts on humanitarian grounds. Phillip Rhodes, who was until recently professor of gynaecology at St Thomas's Hospital Medical School, London, says that while obstetricians have a part to play in reducing the incidence of retardation, they should think very care-fully about it. Having first asked yourself whether a mongol child is completely valueless, you must then ask yourself whether it would be right to rope in all the mothers and cause a great deal of alarm and anxiety to find your one mongol foetus. It's an impossible equa-tion: you prevent an abnormal child but you create thousands of troubled mothers. At Queen Mary's Hospital, Carshalton, where more than 100 mongol children have been admitted for long-term care over the past 10 years, the consultant psychiatrist Dr Brian Kirman says that so far he has yet to meet a parent of a mongol child who would have continued with the pregnancy had they known. But other doctors have never had to cope with mongolism, and never had a patient with a spina bifida child. Others traditionally are slow to recognise and use new techniques. Perhaps they do not realise that the mental and physical strain on a family with a severely handicapped child can sometimes be so enormous that parents often become ill themselves. Which must cause doctors to ask themselves whether they can really afford not to spread the word about their early warning system.'

Financial resources and manpower. With more and more announcements concerning the Government's cuts in Capital Grants, it is difficult to see how research findings can be put into practice. The research/practice gap is that between what research needs to be met and what the local authority is prepared to do about it! In the Harrow project when the needs of the mentally handicapped are established there is little likelihood of there being financial help to provide all the facilities required. Could nurses implement the findings of research if there were only two nurses to cope with the duties of a ward of thirty-five patients? Would nurses who have seen little or no progress in their patients, feel it was worth trying out new ideas that had emerged from research work? Nurses felt unable to do much about their patients when the ward was overcrowded and staff were short. The attitude was one of 'What can two nurses do for thirty-five patients' not one of 'Well, there are thirty-seven people in this ward and we can all interact and help one another'.

Palm Court. The interesting phenomena of Palm Court was described. The residents of this 120-bed hotel are largely ex-subnormality hospital patients. The hotel itself is run by a business woman who has little or no previous experience with the mentally handicapped. Amongst other things she has taught her residents to take their own laundry to the local launderette and has solved her problems concerning the mixed sexes by putting males on one floor and females on the next. If anyone steps out of line it is usually the other residents who sort out the problem!

Is there a gap? Is it true that there is a research/practice gap? Research was much closer to practice than in, say, the field of bio-medicine where there is a time lag of about five years. No clear distinction had been made between the different types of research under discussion. There was little or no research/practice gap in the area of operational research where the research is applied while it is being done. Research on genetics was applied almost instantaneously in the Genetic Counselling Centres that exist. The implication that it was the researchers' fault that their findings were not put into practice gave a false picture. They were concerned to see their research findings applied but if they put them into practice their skills as researchers would be wasted for long periods of time. When distinguished research workers were invited to action workshops to talk to people who would be putting their findings into practice, a very high success rate had been achieved. These distinguished people, with already heavily booked diaries, were willing to give up valuable time to come and help convey the research message to practitioners. In training people to carry out and put into practice research findings, however, there was a gap. It may be necessary for researchers to convey their findings to practitioners in a University setting where the researcher can continue with research and teach at the same time.

A more meaningful classification. Perhaps more could be done about the research/practice gap if a meaningful classification could be devised. The mentally handicapped are all individuals and require different services and facilities. The term 'Mentally Handicapped' does not indicate this range of need.

Bridges under construction

Statutory bridges

In the re-organised National Health Service the appointment in certain areas of specialists in community medicine – attached to social service departments – provides for the co-ordination of advice and planning for all services, including those for the mentally ill and mentally and physically handicapped. Duties also include instituting research and looking at the many different aspects of the services to provide advice to local authorities, the Area Health Authority, Health Care Planning Teams and the District Community Physician. In fact the role is one of integration. There are also the important links of communication between the Department of Health and Social Security and field workers. Ministers are very much aware that it is insufficient to publish statements of general policy. They are very well aware of the need to communicate these policies effectively to field authorities. The Department now has branches linking directly to each Regional Health Authority and these have been set up to improve the communication flow between the Department and the field and equally importantly between the field and the Department. The Department's Regional Social Work Services organisation provides similar links in the social services field. The upheaval of NHS and Local Government re-organisation has meant these agencies have been under considerable pressure and they have yet to experience 'normal' working. The need to ensure efficient communication of policy to the field authorities is however well appreciated by them and by the Department generally.

Independent bridges

The Institute for Research into Mental and Multiple Handicap can be seen as an 'interface' between research and practice. The Institute for Research into Mental Retardation was set up by the National Society for Mentally Handicapped Children eight years ago as an independent charity. It is now 'loosely associated' with the Spastics Society hence its change of name to the Institute for Research into Mental and Multiple Handicap. It has a specialised library for those of post-graduate level and is provided for, and used largely by, research workers. This libraty also forms the basis for answering enquiries at all levels of research. Information ranges from research on genetics to basic research in the medical sciences through to research on service provision. The Institute also tries to keep in contact with researchers in the field. Recently, the Institute have been producing monthly bulletins listing articles published during the previous month. Within a year the subject headings have jumped from just 10 in number to 50. There is a plan to expand this service and produce short summaries of articles and publish them in a form similar to the National Children's Bureau's 'Spotlight series'. The Institute's second function is that of stimulating and co-ordinating research itself. It organises research conferences and discussions. These are usually multi-disciplinary. It also organises Action Workshops when some particularly urgent problem arises of how to put research findings into practice. For instance the antenatal diagnosis of spina bifida or the training of non-psychologists in the use of behaviour modification. The Institute also runs conferences and seminars for health visitors, social workers, doctors, etc. Research findings are brought, in simple terms, to those working in the field. A recent example of this is a conference entitled 'Prevention of Mental Handicap Through Antenatal Care'.

Castle Priory College provides short in-service training courses for those actually working with the handicapped. This College, run by the Spastics Society, provides courses which bring research findings to those working with the handicapped. Courses range from those entitled 'Recent Advances in the Teaching of Multihandicapped Children' to 'Music for the Handicapped – Introductory Course'.

The Personal Social Services Council has only recently been launched. Its role is still not completely clear because of its position in, what is already, quite a congested field. The Council owes its origin to recommendations in the Seebohm Committee's report that a single new advisory council should be established to provide advice to Ministers in the personal social services field. The Council was set up by Sir Keith Joseph in 1973 as an independent body with advisory, research and development functions. It became operational in March 1974. The Council has assumed responsibilities formerly undertaken by the Advisory Councils concerned with child care and physical disability. Its remit is to advise

Ministers on policy issues and to provide suitable information and guidance. It will also promote the development of the personal social services. The Council is an independent body since the greater flexibility afforded by independent status was considered useful in a new and developing field. Finance for the Council is provided jointly by central government and local authorities. While much of its work will relate to governmental responsibilities, the Council hopes also to be a resource for the voluntary movement. The Chairman is Lord James of Rusholme, until recently Vice-Chancellor of the University of York, and the Vice-Chairman is Councillor R. W. G. Humphreys of the London Borough of Camden. The twenty-seven members, formally appointed by Ministers, are drawn from public bodies, local authorities, the professions, the voluntary movement, universities and other institutions. It is unlikely that the Council will ever have a large staff – perhaps ultimately between 20 and 30. Many of the Council's administrative, advisory and intelligence functions will be performed in association with a range of existing organisations. The Council has a direct relationship with government departments, the local authority associations, professional bodies and the Central Council for Education and Training in Social Work. The Council wishes to be accessible and responsive to all who are interested in the personal social services. It has embarked upon a series of consultations throughout the country, in order to develop working relationships with policy-makers, adminstrators and practitioners. Among its early priorities are enquiries, through Working Groups, into standards of residential care and into consumer participation. Manpower planning, the provision of information services and the development of community involvement are among other immediate interests.

An important part of the Council's work will relate to research and it has set up a Research Committee under the chairmanship of Professor David Donnison. The research functions will include: the production of 'current awareness' material dealing with innovation and practical developments; the special study of particular problems; the dissemination of research findings which have a bearing on policies and practices in the personal social services, and the monitoring of research proposals in an attempt to clarify research priorities and strategies. The emphasis is upon disseminating information about research and helping to coordinate the research effort in this field, rather than upon conducting long-term or large-scale projects. Nevertheless, it is hoped to make a useful contribution to knowledge in selected fields and several projects have been initiated. For example, studies of the supply, demand and staffing aspects of residential care will complement the Working Group enquiry. Similarly, the Council's interest in consumer participation will generate research in this field. Other topics, such as the interaction of the personal social services with other social and public services, will be studied. The Council recognises that it will have many responsibilities to discharge at a time when there is growing recognition of the importance of the personal social services – whether among children, young families, the handicapped, the disadvantaged or the elderly – and of their relationship to other major services, notably health, education, housing, income, maintenance and planning.

Other ways of bridging the gap

A central registry? In order for researchers to benefit from the work of others in the field some mechanism, such as a Central Registry of research findings, would be beneficial. For example, the findings of research work done on group homes in, say, the North-West may be very useful as a guide to somebody about to embark on a similar project in the South-East of the country. There was also the need to co-ordinate, not duplicate, these information services and for people to make an effort to pool their work and findings into a National System. The problem of confidentiality and non-popularity may arise. Perhaps a group of people should be specifically appointed, similar to the Agricultural Advisory Service, who would collect and give out information by visiting various organisations who might call on the group for help. The Health Education Council used the techniques of advertising through the media in order to get different messages over to the public.

Marketing research findings. The communication of research findings to those working in the field may be successful. However it is implementation of these findings that is all important. An example was given of how research was marketed in the commercial world. If a research project produces a new kind of soap then the media is mobilised into action. A wrapping, fragrance, shape are all conjured up on the screen, on posters and in the shops so that before long the purchaser cannot visualise buying or using any other soap. What can we learn from this marketing approach in the field of mental handicap?

Motivation. When nurses in a subnormality hospital have seen little or no improvement in their patients over the years it is hard to convince staff that the application of new research findings would greatly help their seemingly unhelpable patients. An experiment was described, conducted by Dr F. Morgenstern, whose nursing staff expected no more from their patients than the daily routine of feeding, coping with incontinence and seeing them sitting day after day in the same places along the same walls. After Dr Morgenstern had different geometrical designs painted on different walls of the wards they realised the potential of their patients who did not remain in their same seats as before but moved to different positions according to their likes and dislikes of the geometrical patterns facing them! Nurses should be stimulated and their potentialities liberated.

Discussion. Although a hospital had tried to introduce a training programme in behaviour modification twice, it was not until recently for the third time – when the climate was right – that the programme was accepted. It is not until a crisis occurs that people exhibit 'information seeking behaviour'. There was a need to deliver information at the point of the problem; to tie up the time scale of need for information and the provision of information. If you are marketing a product you must believe in what you are trying to sell. We need more research into how one gets this belief before we can attempt to market the product. For example, the necessity of convincing employers of the need to employ the mentally handicapped. Concerning the marketing approach, it is very necessary to back this approach up with training for those who will actually be implementing the findings.

Training. In five or ten years the training situation will be different. The General Nursing Council has changed its training for nurses of the mentally handicapped. There is a move away from the idea that the nurse has a purely custodial role, to the idea that she, or he, should stimulate his or her patient and emphasis is put on patients going to work .However, many newly trained nurses are fighting a 'rear-guard' action against the 'die-hard' attitude of older nurses. A similar situation often occurs in adult training centres where younger, trained staff are also fighting a 'rear-guard' action. It is usually the younger, trained managers who are much more enlightened as leaders and have good results.

Finance. If research findings were to be put into practice it would be necessary to get through to the 'purse strings'. There is a great need to motivate local authorities and their policy and resources committees into the need for untying their purse strings and allowing money to be spent on worthwhile projects. If the money is not available then there are always research projects of a less costly nature, or we can put into practice the findings of research that has already been done.

Implementation through action research. Those who are going to implement research findings are those working at the 'grass roots'. Often it is the parents who will implement these findings. Work is being carried out at Barts and Warley Hospitals where visits are made to the homes of the mentally handicapped to see how research findings can be introduced into the home environment. Researchers should not only be researching but also implementing their own findings. This is only possible if research is designed in a certain way so that researcher also become implementers. An example was given of the low success-rate of implementing a very good piece of research. The work of the Ministry of Health which lead in 1965 to a circular on improving the effectiveness of the hospital service for the mentally subnormal was very constructive but very few seemed to act on its recommendations. One must, therefore, influence the people who should take notice and can implement the findings. Action research is one way of doing just this.

Combining research with action. Antagonism comes from some people when they are faced with the possibility of change and when the proposed changes are based on research evidence; some of the responsibility for action and monitoring of outcome lies with the researchers. For example, when a research project is carried out at the request of an institution it is important that the resulting report should be made available to all levels within the institution and not just the higher levels who may choose to see that it goes no further – and this condition should be made before the research is undertaken. Secondly, there is the kind of research activity ongoing in Wessex, where the initial work carried out by Tizard into child-oriented and institution oriented management practices is being put into practice and the problems of doing this are being examined by research workers. Similarly, the practice of teaching the mentally handicapped using new principles can be looked at by the researcher in a hospital setting, where staff training, staff ratios, level of resources available, management practices etc. can be examined as research variables. Also the questions of how staff can be sufficiently motivated to carry on once the period of research is over must be examined. The researcher should join the practitioner in action and the practitioner should also learn to use the techniques of the researcher i.e. systematic observation and record-keeping, *so that* instead of a gap we have an overlap.

At the same time journalists are needed to give widespread publication of recent ideas and thinking so that the interests and openness to change exists among practitioners. To say that there is no research practice gap for which researchers have any responsibility is to ignore a large and fruitful area of valid research activity which should be combined with action.

The Session Editor writes:

It is not easy for a specialist in one field to attend a meeting of specialists in a totally different field and to derive from the discussion some general conclusions which will satisfy those specialists. The interesting fact for me, however, about this particular information Exchange Session was the way in which some general ideas emerged (or, at least, partly emerged) which are a feature not only of the field of mental handicap but also of many other fields. Firstly, there is the difficulty of identifying what is meant by research in an area which involves the interaction of a number of different systems – central government policy, local authority services, health services, education, voluntary services, etc. – and different levels of research activity from basic research in genetics to the evaluation of services. The meeting never quite got to grips with this question which is basic to any consideration of communication in a problem-oriented, multi-disciplinary field.

Arising out of this first aspect of the problem are the following points:—

(1) Is there a need for closer coordination of research than appears to exist at present in this field? The opinion of participants on this point was divided: some felt that in certain areas research could well cease until the results of previous research had been applied, others felt that coordination was unnecessary because the range of problems and research environments was so great that overlap was unlikely. The basis of this division of opinion seemed to lie in the nature of the research referred to – a point which was not clearly established.

(2) Is the problem one of a need for research to be cumulative rather than of a need for coordination? Some participants clearly felt that research ought to build on what had gone before and that in relation to some aspects of mental health this was not happening. It was pointed out, however, that in relation to the genetic basis of mental handicap research *was* cumulative.

(3) In a field of this kind the boundaries between research, development, and application are hazy. This causes some problems of definition but can have beneficial effects in that, particularly in relation to service delivery, research programmes can be devised which embody all three stages. Ali Baquer, P. Isherwood and Mr and Mrs Race all described projects with some element of this integration.

The information communication aspects of the 'research/practice gap' received relatively little attention during the Session but some points can be made. Firstly, some participants questioned whether there was a gap at all, in the information transfer sense. Here again the nature of the research and the field of research seemed to be critical factors. There was general agreement that information transfer among research workers in the same discipline was satisfactory and presented no real problems: what the formal system of publication and abstracting could not give access to, the informal system of direct communication with colleagues could.

Communication between disciplines and between research workers and practitioners could present problems, however, and a variety of techniques was suggested for improving the situation:

(1) more and better reviews of research written for the practitioner and for the layman rather than for fellow research workers;

(2) a central registry of research findings, possibly embodied in a publication such as 'Human behaviour: an inventory of scientific findings' by B. Berelson and G. A. Steiner;

(3) a central advisory service to local authorities and voluntary agencies modelled on the Agricultural Advisory Service; and

(4) closer coordination of the information activities of the numerous voluntary organisations in the field.

In this latter respect would it not be possible to institute a single information bulletin or abstracting service, sponsored by such bodies as the NSMHC and the Institute for Research into Mental and Multiple Handicap, under the auspices of the Personal Social Services Council?

In the end plans for improved research, better information services, and more effective service delivery depend upon the availability of resources. Even in affluent times the social services have never had the level of funding to provide the kinds of services which all practitioners knew to be needed. In the period of shortages, which we seem to be entering, the problems are going to be more acute and the effective communication of ideas, research findings, and practices which work, will be of increasing importance.

T. D. Wilson

Individual contributions are identified by page and line number on the List of Participants. References are identified by page and line, in the same way.

Participants Lists give the name, address, telephone number and post held at the time the contribution was made.

LIST OF PARTICIPANTS

REFERENCES

	page	lines
Revans, R. W. and Baquer, A. 'I thought they were supposed to be doing that' (1972) The Hospital Centre.	121	13
Taylor, D. 'Mental handicap' (1974) The Office of Health Economics.	120	30
Cummings, P. 'Education and the severely handicapped child' (1973) NSMHC.	122	35
Department of Health and Social Security: 'Better services for the mentally handicapped' (1971) Cmnd Paper 4683 HMSO.	122	14
Shennan, V. 'Palm Court revisited' (September 1974) Parent's Voice (Journal of the NSMHC).	126	22
Ministry of Health: 'Improving the effectiveness of the hospital service for the mentally subnormal' (1965) Circular HM(65)104 HMSO.	132	5

CONTINUITY AND CONFIDENTIALITY OF RECORDS

Session Editor: Christina Jolly
Social worker, Royal Borough of Kensington and Chelsea.
Member of the British Association for the Retarded and the Association of
Professions for the Mentally Handicapped

Practical examples

Individual Records. Adults

The Session opened with a practical example of the issues raised. The
proper maintenance of hospital staff records in a Staff Occupational
Health Clinic. It was a simple example, under the control of a single
agency. It left aside the more complex issues raised with respect to
records of mentally handicapped persons.

Every hospital is obliged to employ, in addition to its normal range of
staff, a certain percentage of the disabled and re-habilitated. Some of
these may have past histories of mental illness, health disorders, and
delinquency. The key issues raised were:—

Continuity. What kind of information should be collected?
From whom should it be obtained? For how long should it be kept?

Confidentiality. Who should hold this information? Who should
be allowed to see it? For what purposes should it be used? In the
interests of other staff, and also of the patients, to what extent should
confidentiality be conditional?

Invasion of privacy. From the point of view of the individual
concerned was there any possibility of invasion of privacy? Should an
individual, for example, be allowed to know what his own record
contains? Should he be allowed to comment upon facts, or upon the
uses that are likely to be made of them?

Discussion. It was not possible to consider confidentiality of records
without also having regard to communication. In the practical example
given there was not only the question of from whom the information

139

should be withheld, but also the problem of to whom it should be given – or communicated. It was true that hospitals do not always know what kind of staff they are getting: earlier records may be missing or incomplete: the case of an eighteen year old psychopath and a girl epileptic were quoted. Under NHS reorganisation it will be likely that staff records will be centralised and case sheets will be kept at the new area levels. From these, information can be sifted (with due regard to confidentiality), via reports for the use of those to whom such information is relevant. To protect the individual, some authorities, when engaging staff, tell applicants that full access to their past records will be required: they may therefore, if they so wish, withdraw their application. This leaves the initiative, with regard to privacy, in the hands of the individual concerned. The individual would also be informed, should his application prove to be successful, with whom this information is likely to be shared.

Group casework records

Issues with respect to continuity and confidentiality of records as they might affect practical aspects of social casework were outlined. An example was used of the case of a family under suspicion for the non-accidental damage of one of their children. Records, and the need for continuity and confidentiality, must be seen within the context of the 'end product' of work with a client: that is, the maintenance of records which can benefit the client either present or future. The need for confidentiality of recorded material arises because the client and worker are involved in a sensitive search for reality. As the realities are recognised and tolerated by the client, his freedom to share materials develops. In the meantime, value judgements are required and ethical decisions need to be made as to what is confidential and what is not, to whom, and at what time an occasion reference may be made. Therefore there should be continuing efforts made by worker and client together to divest original confidential relevant material of its secrecy.

Avoiding unnecessary confidentiality. Words that are spoken and thoughts that are shared are not for any purpose other than to help clients: distinction will be made between these words and thoughts that are part of a therapeutic situation, and those that produce a movement or change in 'direction'. This means that the first may be entirely confidential (non-recorded), the second of value for record purposes (open). It is essential to recognise there can be a false premise of confidentiality and this can be due to lazy casework. This can preclude the positive movement of a case, and can cause great trouble in achieving the co-operation of one case-worker with another: a 'wall' of confidentiality. The so-called 'Multi-Disciplinary Approach' has dangers. It will not always be recognised that all of us have a little bit of a 'social worker' tucked away inside us. It is the same with health visitors, psychologists, doctors, nurses, physiotherapists and consultants. The social worker will usually be aware of these many sides of us, since she (or he) will have been trained consciously to switch to each according to activity (say, wife, mother, social worker, administrator, etc.). The other members of a multi-disciplinary team may not have learnt to do this. Therefore, those of the team representing the professional caring skills may simply be speaking as emotive persons, and not limiting themselves to their own professional discipline. From the point of view of record making, continuity of records and actual needs for confidentiality, it is necessary to recognise that social workers are prone to this kind of invasion: this should be recognised and adjustment made.

From confidentiality to non-confidentiality. The necessity for confidentiality will arise when there is a gap between what is thought to be known about a matter, and what is thought to be 'acceptable'. Since much information will exist in the first place only in the client's own mind, and the client will find it difficult to verbalise and understand, at the start much information will be 'confidential' because the only persons in possession of it will be the clients themselves: it will be 'progress' when the client is enabled to 'recognise' this information and share it with a social worker: at this stage progress will have been made, but the information will clearly be confidential to both client and worker. As, in the process, 'directions' emerge for possible action, so also will the client's acceptance of the fact that, for the benefit of himself, the family, or the child, such 'directions' can only be achieved by overcoming feelings about confidentiality, so that such information may then be applied. For example, Mrs Bloggs agrees, say, to allowing the warden of the hostel to which Johnny is being sent to share information about (say) the reason for his need for residential care. There will therefore be liberation of some material from confidentiality depending upon 'directions' and on the passage of time. There will also be a need for specialised reports that can be handed on, not detailed, but sufficient to indicate that Mrs Bloggs has an area of anxiety, and that perhaps, more information might follow later.

Avoiding the 'punitive'. Of special importance (as regards confidentiality) is the need to consider what may be called 'threatening information': that is, the apparent 'punitive' aspects of records. For example, at a multi-disciplinary conference it is seen that parents under suspicion for the non-accidental damage of one of their children are thought (both mother and father) to be severe psychopaths. There may be need for 'a place of safety order' for the child, and need to consider other siblings. Work on a case like this may be seen as 'punitive' unless there is proper diagnosis of the parents' psychiatric condition and the case is shown to be moving in a 'sharing' direction: that is, that the parents should if possible (in due course) be helped to understand their condition on which the residential care of their child is based (supposing they 'burn' out at forty – and the immediate management of the case can be seen not as 'punitive' but as a means of making the family able to re-assemble at a later date). Here both continuity of records, and confidentiality, are vital factors, and can only arise from balanced ethical/functional decisions. For example in a case of this kind, a number of the multi-disciplinary team could not understand why an attempt at a positive diagnosis of the parents needed to be made, yet the long-term outcome of this kind of case rests upon this being done, and records being kept, many of which will remain confidential until such time as they can be 'communicated' to care staff – to foster-parents – or to the parents themselves.

Shock deafness. 'Shock deafness' means that you may not communicate – although you gave information – to a client. There is also the 'deafness' that can arise from one kind of discipline trying to communicate with another. Records – their continuity – and their confidentiality – will be of little use unless they are concerned – not with what was said – but the extent to which it was understood, accepted, and made the means of new 'directions'.

Model projects

Project one

Record keeping. In a paper Mrs Sandhya Naidoo, Senior Research Officer, National Children's Bureau had suggested that record keeping systems (for children) are numerous and diverse but even where there is some uniformity of purpose wide variations are found. This suggestion followed recommendations that a national form of record card should be devised; a suggestion supported by the Seebohm Committee. Mrs Naidoo's Paper presented some of the issues involved in developing new record keeping systems in the fields of child care, health and education. A National Children's Bureau current Development Record Project was described. A record system to chart children's development is being devised by a Research Team for use by those who have daily contact with children in situations which allow detailed knowledge of them. An experimental form of a developmental record chart for 0–5 year olds will shortly be completed and is concerned with their social, emotional, linguistic, cognitive and motor functioning. The preparatory work on a record for children in the age-range 5–9 years is now under way. Later this will be extended for use with older children.

Aims of the developmental chart. To provide an objective means, through a system of carefully guided observations, for indicating in functional terms how children are developing. To reveal, by completion at regular intervals, progress over a period of months or years as desirable. To provide insight into developmental delay and reveal areas of special need. To provide information which will form a basis for planning and executing measures to meet the needs of individual children. To provide a long-term record of development.

Project two

Record maintenance and management. There was not only a real need for the proper standardisation of record-keeping procedures; effective communication between agencies and professions, both statutory and voluntary, was also of vital importance. In the absence of Dr C. Simpson Smith, MB, BS, MRCS, LRCP, FFCM, a Principal Medical Officer, West Riding County Council, details of a project, started in 1964 were tabled. It was thought these might become the basis for a comprehensive child health record-keeping system (using a computer for information storage). The aim of this project was (1) To establish continuity of records. (2) To ensure uniform ascertainment of handicap. (3) To aid co-ordination of services. (4) To predict future services needed for individual children. (5) To provide planning data. (6) To facilitate research. Notifications (from Health Visitors, etc.) are now more uniform and of better quality: of particular interest is the breakdown of defect by diagnosis; active cases were as follows: spina bifida 319; cystic fibrosis 29; hearing loss 603; moderately subnormal 2,779; severely subnormal 765.

Approaches to good practice

Individual records

It was often presumed that the more we know the more we can help. This was not so. There was sometimes a compulsion to try to know all: this must be avoided. The following suggestions were made:

Emotion and intuition. Records tend to be based on reason and logic; work with people depends also upon emotion and intuition. This can play a crucial part.

Bias. That allowance should be made for personal bias in both the selection and presentation of recorded information. This bias can also apply to the reading and interpretation of records. This bias will be partly innate, partly cultural and will also be due to other factors operating upon the observer/recorder/reader.

Infinite variety. It was not possible to evolve a method of record-keeping which can satisfy all. Different information is required by different people at different times, for an infinite variety of purposes.

Good records a compromise. Good records will always be a compromise. They will be factual: opinion, if included at all, will be shown as such.

Brevity. The value of records will often depend, in particular, upon their brevity: the longer they take to read, the less likely they are to be read.

Group (casework) records

Particular concern was expressed with regard to effective communication; between client and worker: between discipline and discipline: between agency and agency. There was also the problem of the multiplicity of agencies, each dealing with different phases in the life of a mentally handicapped person. Whilst this fragmentation will clearly be avoided in the future by more effective record-keeping (see Model One, page 142) and by the more effective continuity and standardisation of record management (see Model Two, page 143), not only did these not yet exist, but the problem was exacerbated to a dangerous extent by many features: (for example, the multi-disciplinary confusion of roles). Studies had shown that there was not only considerable misunderstanding in respect of their own roles and responsibilities by the professions concerned with the mentally handicapped; there is also confusion in the roles and responsibilities they attributed to their colleagues. It was unfortunate that the Seebohm re-organisation had come before the introduction of effective record-keeping systems; there was also the upheaval associated with the re-organisation of the National Health Service. Reports on the implications of these changes have recently been published with regard to the school-age mentally handicapped; also the impact upon hospital records and co-ordination of services. There is also an edited version of a recent Symposium on information services at which problems were reported and discussed.

Pre-Seebohm days. In pre-Seebohm days with relatively permanent staff in small specialised departments, workers could carry their 'records' in their heads: they were also available for advice and consultation with their colleagues in other agencies, and in other disciplines. Nowadays the generic approach, to which must be added the very high turnover of younger workers moving from place to place, due to career advancement, marriage and housing shortage means that the maintenance of reliable and continuous records has become crucial. Under the circumstances two situations have been known to arise, both of them avoidable. Families, or individual clients, can reach 'breaking-point' and it is only when a state of crisis has arisen that their situation comes to the surface. These are often the people who 'try to manage'. At the other end of the scale are the many families who 'scream loudest' and tend to take advantage of services. Without effective records the distribution of time given to these cases cannot be planned. Before Seebohm many of these families would have been known to workers over a period of time. This is no longer the case. It is for this reason that effective records, and effective communication have now become a vital need in preventing the breakdown of services to the mentally handicapped and their families. For case histories where services have broken down, see 'Return to Community Life' (page 83).

Bridging the gap, surveys

With regard to the gap which existed between present (urgent) needs, and the prospects offered by developments in the future, various kinds of action could be initiated without need for further delay. There was, for example, the provision by the National Society for these present multi-disciplinary Information Exchange Sessions: these were one aid to bridging the gap between individual workers (and agencies). There were also useful publications: one author includes a bibliography of more than 100 references relating to most of the standard work that has been under-taken in this field. He also provides a useful guide to further reading, specific to the topics raised at this present Information Exchange. In the current absence of effective continuity of records there were also the 'once only' or 'time to time' surveys, largely initiated by local authorities following the 'Chronically Sick and Disabled Persons Act 1970'. In some cases the mentally handicapped were included in these surveys: in some cases they were excluded. The Act was not clear on this issue.

Local surveys. There were, however, the surveys initiated by local societies of the NSMHC. The work of the Greenwich Society in this field was an outstanding example. This report is an 'in depth' survey of mentally handicapped persons at home and in the community. It includes family details and diagnosis, and covers all ages, from children under 5 years, the 5 to 16 age group, and those over 16 years of age.

Long term care survey. A survey of patients in long term hospital care was described. For this survey a questionnaire has been designed by the London Borough of Greenwich. The particular importance of this questionnaire is not only that it is designed for completion by a variety of possible disciplines that may have contact with the long-stay patient: it also enables the member of staff concerned to pursue new lines of activity in relation to the needs of the patient that are disclosed to them in the process of completing the questionnaire. The variety of possible disciplines for which the use of this questionnaire is designed include medical staff, nursing staff, psychologist, social worker, teacher, occupational therapist, speech therapist, industrial unit staff, and others.

Government's statement. On the day prior to the Information Exchange the hope had been expressed in the House of Commons that the Government might consider the value of survey methods (such as the present examples given), in bridging the present gap in the continuity of records as they affect the mentally handicapped. The Secretary of State, through Dr David Owen, announced her refusal to consider this.

Mr Kenneth Clarke asked: 'Whether the Secretary of State will carry out a survey into or make an estimate of the number of adult mentally handicapped in need of hostel, community home, or other residential sheltered accommodation in each county of England and Wales'.

Dr David Owen, on behalf of the Secretary of State replied: 'A mentally handicapped person's need for residential accommodation depends upon the extent to which support facilities are available. In general local authorities are reasonably well informed about the number and the needs of the mentally handicapped in their areas, and I do not think a general survey on this subject would be appropriate at the present time. Very detailed surveys undertaken in limited areas have played, and will continue to play, an important part in developing mental handicap policy'.

Confidentiality

It was reported that confidentiality in social work had been the topic of a number of publications by the British Association of Social Workers and that the Association's Working Party on Confidentiality had formulated questions designed to be asked by social workers, about his agency, his client, and himself.

Individual records. In the example given with regard to hospital staff records (page 139) it had been pointed out that there was no such thing as absolute confidentiality, unless you put your records in a safe and throw away the key! Even a priest can talk in his sleep! Confidentiality must be a conditional matter (in this specific example) and must be largely based on trust in people; this will often depend upon the kind of structure of the organisation concerned; on whether, for example, they are Goffman-like. Goffman suggests that, in a bad 'institution' of any kind, be it barracks, hospital, school (or hostel) . . . there is a split between a managed group, conveniently called inmates, and a small supervisory group. Each group tends to conceive of the other in hostile stereotypes.

The supervisory group see the inmates as bitter, secretive and untrustworthy. The inmates see the supervisory group as condescending, high-handed and mean. Social mobility between the two groups is grossly restricted. Social distance is typically great, and often formally prescribed. It was noted that contrasts between small 'institutions' and large ones had also been suggested. In the large institution there will be many departments: each may differ in their degree of autonomy: there will therefore be freedom for individual units to avoid the 'institutional' setting. A small unit will usually be under a single management; if it is good, it is good; if bad, very bad. In any good organisation the principle of people trusting each other was of paramount importance.

Casework records. Reference was made to the special nature of the client/worker/agency relationship and the work of Timms, where the role of the social worker is seen as a substitute for the traditional support of the extended family. Particular consideration was required to meet client needs in a society where there was increasingly family dispersion, absence of friend and trusted neighbour (from the rural to urban society), and the need, for many, for what was in practice a substitute for a wholly trustworthy friend and confidant. With regard to confidentiality, the issues involved, particularly in situations of crisis, were complex, and required much further study. Basically an essential feature was the participation of the client in all issues seen to involve confidentiality. The client must be consulted, and, whenever possible, permission for disclosure must be obtained; but the client must also understand the nature, and the need for, the permission for which he was being asked. From this there also follows the problems arising where the exceptions to client permission may – or must – apply. For example, danger to themselves, or others, but this again qualified by certain conditions and circumstances. There was then the problem of where responsibility for decision-making of these kinds rested; with social workers, with senior colleagues, with directors – perhaps even with the government departments who were responsible for the services concerned. There was also the problem of 'presumed permission'.

A code of ethics: Practical implications. With regard to the BASW proposed Code of Ethics a further modified document was under discussion at present with the BMA, and would be published in due course. There was, however, an aspect of the legal and ethical responsibility which was fundamental. Would social workers be prepared to accept the principle, as it applies to the medical profession; that they be expelled from the Association, in the event of a charge of non-professional conduct (according to the Code) having been proven against them?

Presenting self

Was there a special case – even a unique case – in respect of continuity and confidentiality of records, presented by children and adults who suffer mental handicap?

In the Session 'Employment' (page 99) special attention had been drawn to the need for continuity and completeness of records. In the Session on 'Social Training and Social Competence' (page 71) the danger of 'crude guesses' had been emphasised. With regard to placement in an Adult Training Centre, a Careers Officer had said: ('Employment': page 99).

'The mixture of old and young, of degrees of disability, and of kinds of personality difficulty can often lead to a depressing and defeatist labelling of the whole group as 'the mentally handicapped'. Prospects for the individual human being can be lost under such circumstances.'

Whilst it may be necessary to generalise, for the purposes of argument and exchange of information, we must all try to avoid the 'all or nothing' syndrome: that is, treating generalisations as if they were true. For example, the notion that 'all policemen are the same' is likely to be disproved if they are asked to take off their helmets! At least one of them will have red hair!

Records should be used to individuate – not to categorise. For adults this principle was of even more importance. Without proper continuity of records the unique identity of an individual can be lost. It is therefore not possible to accord to them the rights to which, as citizens, they are entitled. This is mainly because they lack the capacity to undertake for themselves the presentation of self in everyday life. For this they have to rely on others. Confidentiality, and communication, were mutually exclusive. Therefore, if records did not exist, or were not known to exist, how can help be given to those who rely on us to mediate for them? The term 'the mentally handicapped' was a generalisation. Even the so-called categories of 'subnormal' and 'severely subnormal' were bogus, since there was a continuum that ran from one end of the scale to the other – from the gifted to those of the lowest intelligence. But if we are to talk about services and provisions – or records and confidentiality – some generalisations have to be made. Poor records, and the use of unnecessary confidentiality, could defeat the attempts of agencies (and individuals) to secure for the mentally handicapped their rights as individuals.

The Session Editor writes:

As this Session progressed I felt that we all believed that information entrusted to us by our clients could be used in a variety of ways, so long as the full co-operation of the client was sought as problems were brought to light.

That occasionally, we may be put into the position of breaking confidence if there was evidence of danger to the client, the worker, other people, the community or the agency. But this only in relation to the needs of a certain situation at a particular moment in time.

A client or patient who requests help will invariably allow other resources, apart from ourselves and our own agencies, to be brought into use to try to solve particular problems as they arise, so long as we are absolutely honest in all our communications – this implies implicit trust – the faith of the client/patient in us, and our trust in the client – it is a two-way process!

We must also be absolutely sure that the client understands what is happening. When a situation is too traumatic a human being is so shocked that he often hears very little of what is discussed with him and although information has been given to the client, there has been no actual communication as he had not heard.

Then this Information Session highlighted for me, and I think for everyone, the truth, that the actual meaning of the word 'confidential', from the Latin is, 'with trust'. I, therefore, feel that we might well use the word 'trust' in our minds, instead of the linguistically overwhelming word 'confidentiality'. Trust in relation to the retarded is a rather sacred concept, not to be taken lightly, or disregarded, if we cannot, or do not, comprehend their degree of ability to trust, or be trusted, because of their retardation.

Continuity, I felt, the participants found difficult, especially those in agencies where there was a large turnover of staff who never seemed to stay in a situation long enough to really know their clients. This led us on to records and how these could possibly remedy this lack in communication which in the past seemed to be written in a worker's mind as well as on paper.

But the sands of time run out on us and having delved into deep waters we were left on the shore with immense areas around us which we still wished to explore. Every one of us, I felt, would like a Session devoted to good practice in relation to records, so that perhaps in the future comprehensive records could easily show what was happening at a glance, without taking away the feeling quality of the process.

I myself, when first requested to be the Editor of this Session, wondered in what this position would involve me. I was told that apart from checking all the material for the Report before it was finally printed, I was to be a 'good listener' and a professional presence at the actual Session. I felt very honoured to be chosen by the Society and was pleased to accept.

I found that I was extremely stimulated by the participants and felt their immense concern within the areas we discussed and exchanged views.

I was also impressed by their honesty in all areas of discussion, related perhaps to the warmth of personalities which emanated from this small group of people. I would therefore like to extend my sincere thanks to everyone for making my task so pleasant and anxiety free. I loved every minute of this lively Session and hope I adequately fulfilled the role prescribed.

Christina Jolly

Individual contributions are identified by page and line number on the List of Participants. References are identified by page and line, in the same way.

Participants Lists give the name, address, telephone number and post held at the time the contribution was made.

LIST OF PARTICIPANTS

REFERENCES

	page	*lines*

NAIDOO, S. 'Record keeping' Summer (1972) Concern: The Journal of the National Children's Bureau. — 142, 25

SCOTTISH ADVISORY COMMITTEE ON CHILD CARE: 'Handicapped children in care of local authority and voluntary organisations' (1970) Edinburgh HMSO. — 142, 27

DEPARTMENT OF HEALTH AND SOCIAL SECURITY: 'Report of committee on local authority and allied personal social services' (The Seebohm Report) (1968) HMSO. — 142, 27

SMITH, C. SIMPSON (and co-authors) 'Handicap defect register' (July 14 1973) Health and Social Service Journal. — 143, 15

REVANS, R. W. and BAQUER ALI: 'I thought they were supposed to be doing that' (A comparative study of co-ordination of services for the mentally handicapped in seven local authority areas) (1972) The Hospital Centre. London. — 144, 23

DEPARTMENT OF EDUCATION AND SCIENCE: Administrative Memorandum: 'Future arrangements for the handling of school health service records and statistical returns' (26 March, 1974) DES 2/74. — 144, 29

DEPARTMENT OF HEALTH AND SOCIAL SECURITY: 'Organisation of medical work in hospitals' (Third report of a joint working party) (1974) HMSO. — 144, 29

DEPARTMENT OF HEALTH AND SOCIAL SECURITY: Health Services 1 Division: 'Report of symposium on information services' (Limited supply only direct from DHSS). — 144, 32

DAY, PETER: 'Communication in social work' London (1972) Pergamon Press (See Chapter: 'The community, the social agency and the social worker'). — 145, 21

THE GREENWICH SOCIETY FOR MENTALLY HANDICAPPED CHILDREN: 'Travelling hopefully' (A survey). — 145, 30

THE LONDON BOROUGH OF GREENWICH: 'Services for the mentally handicapped in the London borough of Greenwich' (1975). — 146, 5

HOUSE OF COMMONS 'Hansard' (10 April 1974) HMSO. — 146, 12

THE BRITISH ASSOCIATION OF SOCIAL WORKERS: 'Discussion Paper No. 1. Confidentiality in social work' (1974). — 146, 28

THE BRITISH ASSOCIATION OF SOCIAL WORKERS: 'Discussion Paper No. 2. A code of ethics for social work' (1974). — 146, 28

GOFFMAN, E. 'Asylums' (1961) Archer Books and Co. Inc. New York. — 147, 4

MILLER, E. J. and ANYONE, G. V. 'A life apart' (1972) Lippincott. London Tavistock Publications. — 147, 10

MAYER, J. E. and TIMMS, N. 'The client speaks' (1970) London. Routledge and Kegan Paul. — 147, 15

WOLFENSBERGER, W. 'Normalisation' (1972) National Institute for Mental Retardation (Sponsored by the Canadian Association for the Mentally Retarded). — 148, 20

GOFFMAN, E. 'The presentation of self in everyday life' (1956) Edinburgh University Press. — 148, 24

AXLINE, V. 'Dibs — in search of self' (1964) Pelican. — 148, 24

ROGERS, C. 'On becoming a person' (1967) Constable. — 148, 24